The Greatest Cars

The Greatest Cars

by Ralph Stein

A Ridge Press Book

✳

Simon and Schuster

Editor-in-Chief: Jerry Mason
Editor: Adolph Suehsdorf
Art Director: Harry Brocke
Associate Art Director: Harry Redler
Associate Editor: Ronne Peltzman
Art Associate: Nancy Mack
Art Associate: Liney Li
Art Production: Doris Mullane
Production Consultant: Arthur Gubernick

Grateful acknowledgment is made to the
following sources: G. T. Foulis & Co. Ltd., Haynes Publishing Group,
for permission to quote from *Split Seconds* by Raymond Mays;
Faber and Faber Ltd., Publishers, for permission
to quote from *Those Bentley Days* by A. F. C. Hillstead;
The Hamlyn Publishing Group Ltd., for permission to quote
from *A Racing Motorist* by S. C. H. Davis.

THE GREATEST CARS

Published in 1979 by Simon and Schuster
A Division of Gulf & Western Corporation
Simon & Schuster Building
Rockefeller Center
1230 Avenue of the Americas
New York, New York 10020

Library of Congress Catalog Card Number: 79-87901
ISBN 0-671-25195-3

Printed and bound in the Netherlands
by Smeets Offset, Weert.

For Muriel

Bentley page 130

Hispano-Suiza page 154

Maserati page 170

Isotta Fraschini page 186

Rolls-Royce page 202

Introduction

Of the many marques of motorcar constructed during the past ninety-odd years, a select few have stood above their contemporaries. Some achieved greatness because they were designed by inspired engineers and were built to standards of perfection almost unknown today. The Rolls-Royce, the Hispano-Suiza, and the Duesenberg were such jewels. Others, like the Isotta Fraschini, were of unsurpassed luxuriousness. A revered few, with mechanisms quite as splendidly constructed, also offered high speed and remarkable handling and roadholding. The Bugattis and the Alfa Romeos were second to none among such sporting machines.

The Bentleys, the old pre-Rolls-Royce thunderers, are great not merely because they were fine, fast motorcars but also because of the homage paid to them by generations of old-school-tie Englishmen who just can't forget their victories at Le Mans fifty years ago.

At least one great name, Mercedes-Benz, that combination of the world's most ancient marques, emblazoned its star on some of the most successful racing machines of all time and also built superlative road cars in many guises, from echt supersporting brutes to super-luxury equipages for the conveyance of the superrich.

Some of the "greatest" cars are long gone. Of the old names only Rolls-Royce, Mercedes-Benz, and Alfa Romeo remain alive. They still build cars, but in a world much changed, and the cars they produce are, perforce, much changed, too. For no factory in our time can hire a journeyman at £2 a week to lavish a hundred hours on hand filing and fitting the gear teeth of a differential so that no sound will intrude on the prattle of the duchesses in the rear compartment of a limousine.

Some of these "greatest" cars were by no means great in every respect. The Duesenberg, for example, although a near miracle of construction and, indeed, wonderfully quick for its time, was more suited to the long straight roads of its native American Midwest than to terrain where there were corners to be negotiated. A Duesenberg could not be called nimble. Nor was the Isotta Fraschini the kind of car you'd hurl around a corner. It was not meant to be.

No modern builders of sports cars would dare today to market open supercharged machines like a Type 55 Bugatti or an 8C 2300 Alfa Romeo. Sporting drivers today just aren't Spartan enough to subject themselves to the wind, weather, and noise of such blood-curdling devices. Recently I went out in a Type 55. After ten miles or so I was worn out by the rush of air and the mechanical uproar.

But not all of the "greatest" cars go back to the dear dead days. Ferrari and Maserati have been producing sports cars for only some thirty years, but their names are indubitably right up there with the greats.

Other superior motorcars are not among the chosen few in this perhaps snobbish book. The pre-World War II Lincolns, the Packards of those days, the Delage, the Lancia come to mind, as do names from the distant past—Lanchester, Simplex, Delaunay-Belleville. But I submit that none of these has the mystique, the glamour, or the ability to generate so much emotion in so many kinds of autophiles as do the cars whose biographies we herewith present.

Many people have taken much trouble to help me with the photography in this book. In this country, Mr. Jim Edwards of Harrah's Automobile Collection in Reno, Nevada; Mr. Luigi Chinetti and Mr. Thomas Parker of Chinetti International Motors, in Greenwich, Connecticut; Mr. George A. Garbutt of Maserati Automobiles, Inc.; Mr. A. B. Shuman of Mercedes-Benz of North America, Inc.; Mr. Tony Hogg, editor of Road and Track *magazine; Mr. James A. Bradley, curator of the Automotive History Collection at the Detroit Public Library; Mr. Dieter Holterbosch; Mr. Miles Coverdale; Mr. Theodore Mintz; Mr. William Johnson; Mr. Maurice Schwartz; and Mr. Curtis Blake and his brother Mr. Presley Blake all helped me immeasurably. In England, Mr. D. E. A. Miller-Williams of Rolls-Royce Limited; Lord Montagu of Beaulieu and his National Motor Museum; the Bentley Drivers' Club; and Mr. H. G. Conway gave me inestimable help. I owe them all my sincere gratitude.*

R.S.
Tumbrils' End, Westbrook, Connecticut

Alfa Romeo

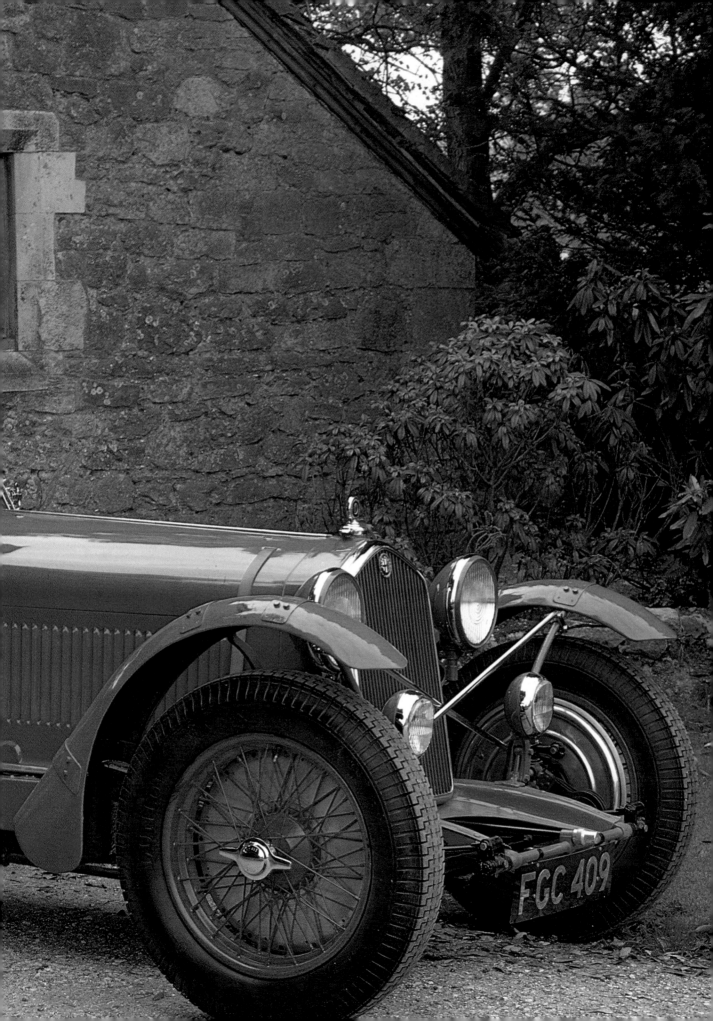

ntil the beginning of World War II, there were two great sports cars: Bugatti and Alfa Romeo. Only the Bugatti equaled the Alfa Romeo and only the Alfa Romeo equaled the Bugatti. The Ferrari, not the present-day Alfa, is the true descendant of the Alfa Romeos as they were in their great days, the fifteen years between 1925 and 1940.

A.L.F.A. (Anonima Lombarda Fabbrica Automobili) built its first car in Milan in 1910. The company was the successor to that founded by Alexandre Darracq, the sharp French automotive entrepreneur, whose attempt to build Italian Darracqs had been a disaster.

The new company, managed by Ugo Stella, who had also directed Darracq's aborted Societa Anonima Italiana Darracq, hired a designer named Giuseppe Merosi, who had a degree not as an engineer but as a surveyor. He had, however, designed bicycles and had worked for Fiat's racing department.

Darracq had attempted to sell some of his rather frail and cheap one- and two-cylinder machines in Italy. These were not only defeated by the steepness of Italy's twisting mountain roads but were also done in by their roughness. Merosi was instructed to design cars tough enough to cope with Italy's antediluvian highways. This he did with a couple of undistinguished models—one a 42-hp, four-cylinder, 4-liter tourer, the other a 24-hp, four-cylinder machine of 2.4 liters. It took until after World War I to get rid of a thousand of these dullards, despite many attempts to improve them.

Someone at A.L.F.A. must have had a lot of gall. In 1911 it was decided that the company ought to go racing to get its cars some publicity. Merosi was to make a racing machine, the 24-hp Corsa, out of that sow's ear, the 24-hp tourer. Two of these lightened, shortened, bucket-seated machines capable of some 70 mph were sent off to do battle in that roughest, toughest of all road races, the Targa Florio in Sicily. That mountain circuit is bad enough today. Imagine what it must have been like in the even more primitive Sicily of 1911. One of the cars driven by Nino Franchini, the factory test driver, led for a while. The other car broke down. But frightful weather conditions finally put both machines out of the race. The following year another Alfa tried again, once more without success. Alfa had begun a tradition of engaging in racing that still continues.

Merosi built other, faster, better machines that were entered in races and hill climbs until Italy found itself at war against Austria and Germany in 1915. With the market for cars gone, Merosi designed a gas-engined generator for military use that, it was hoped, would keep things going for a while.

But Alfa was lucky. A bright young engineer, Nicola Romeo, was looking for manufacturing facilities for his expanding business building military hardware for the government. The Alfa factory was perfect for his purposes,

Preceding pages: 1933 8C 2300 Le Mans-type
Alfa Romeo had a supercharged twin-overhead-camshaft
engine that developed 180 hp at 5,400 rpm. This
two/four-seater driven by Heldé and Stoffel took second place
in the 1935 24-hour Le Mans race. The thick extension
of the rear fender held the battery.

and in 1916 he bought enough Alfa shares to gain control of the company.

War business boomed—trebled and then quadrupled. Alfa ground out airplane engines, railway axles and wheels, tractors. Other factories were gobbled up. Alfa became Alfa Romeo.

Suddenly it was November 11, 1918. The big war contracts dried up. Alfa Romeo went back to building cars, and within a year factory cars started racing again with a fair number of wins.

The first moderately successful postwar touring car was the ES, developed from the prewar 24-hp machine but now with a 4¼-liter four-cylinder engine and capable of about 80 mph, fast for 1921. In sports two-seater form, two of them driven by Alberto Ascari and Ugo Sivocci took first and second places in the Parma-Berceto hill climb in 1921. That year Merosi designed the famous RL model. Its supersports version, the RLSS, would be the first great Alfa Romeo. Before the RLSS appeared in 1925 a sports car, the RLS (S for sport) and the RLTF (TF for Targa Florio) made their bows. The RLTF was, however, made in very small numbers and built mostly for the race whose initials it bore. The RLS was powered by a six-cylinder engine of 2,994 cc that had pushrod overhead valves and a compression ratio of 5.52 to 1. It developed 72 bhp. Eighty mph was attainable. It had a four-speed gearbox whose widely spaced ratios were disliked by sporting drivers, so much so that Alfa's British

dealer offered a substitute transmission with closer ratios. The RLS also had a shorter chassis than the not-too-exciting RL Normale, whose engine had developed a mere 56 bhp.

The RLTF's were quite different beasts. Built for sports-car racing, their light two-seater bodies were mounted on shortened RL chassis frames. Some had engines bored out to 3,620 cc. Their crankshafts whirled on seven main bearings instead of the normal four. They had larger valves than normal and the rev limit was 5,000 instead of the 3,600 rpm of production models. With 125 bhp it was possible to exceed 100 mph.

In 1932 I bought an RLSS 22/90 with a four-passenger touring body. The body bore no maker's name, but I still think it was by Castagna. The car was a 1925 model. It had a pushrod overhead-valve six-cylinder 2,994-cc engine. Originally twin Zenith carburetors had been fitted, but by the time I got the car a previous owner, hoping to get better performance, had installed a pair of American Winfields. Eighty-three bhp was developed. The best speed I ever saw on the clock was 87 mph.

When I first got the car it steered oddly. Take a sharp corner and it balked at straightening up. It wanted to continue turning. Rather frightening. We finally discovered that the wooden wedges that set the caster angle of the front wheels had been set backward on the front axle. After the wedges were turned around, the big Alfa steered beautifully. It was quick and had no lost motion. It needed only two

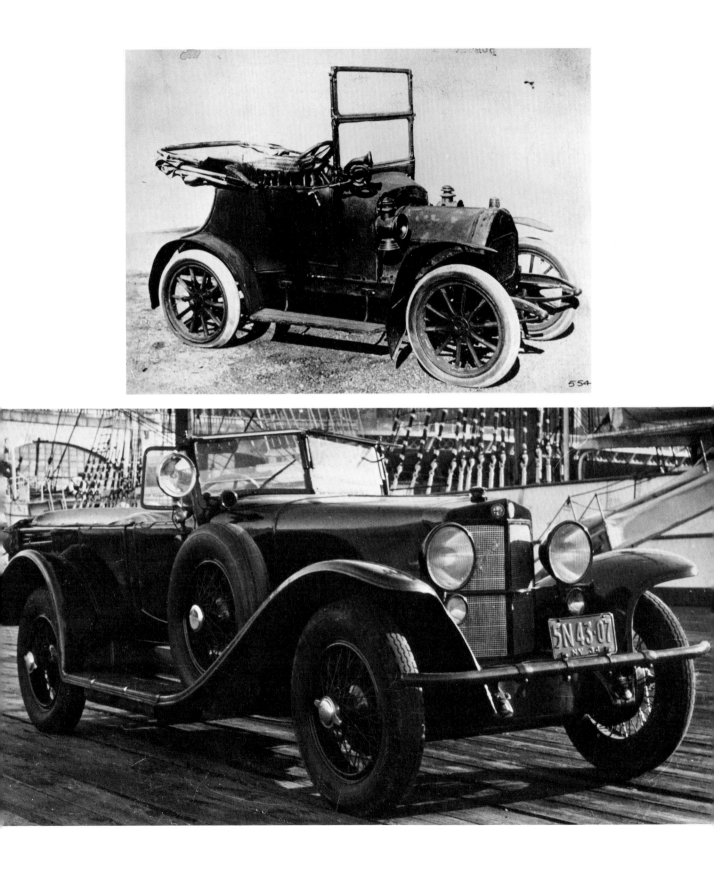

turns to take it from lock to lock. The four gear ratios were a bit peculiar, though, with a big gap between top and third speed. The highest speed obtainable in third was just under 60 mph, so that shifting down from high in order to pass was not too practical. Still, the nonsynchromesh gearbox was not too difficult to manipulate.

The 22/90 had its peculiarities. The engine had dry sump lubrication. The oil—3 gallons of the stuff—was carried in a big tank under the dash right over the knees of the occupants of the front seat. This was filled from above. Although the crankcase still had its own filler and dipstick, these were vestiges from the unsporting RL model and were not supposed to be used on the RLSS. In my ignorance I filled both the crankcase and the oil tank just before I went for my first ride in the Alfa, accompanied by a young lady dressed to the nines for the occasion. For some obscure reason—perhaps because the dashboard tank was unable to cope with the oil under pressure that was pumped from the crankcase—the tank split right above our knees, with dire results.

The 22/90 Alfa had four-wheel brakes. But instead of rods or cables, they were activated by steel tapes. In front the tapes pulled little chains, which then pulled short lengths of cable through the hollow kingpins. These in turn put on the brakes. The hand brake expanded a pair of brake shoes inside a ribbed drum attached to the rear of the gearbox.

Before starting, it was necessary to pump air into the gas tank by means of a pump handle on the dash. When the air gauge read 2 pounds you stopped pumping. After that an engine-driven air pump maintained the pressure.

Lubrication of the chassis was accomplished by means of a Tecalemit grease gun, the kind that slid onto the flat nipples. There were no such guns to be had in the United States. At least I couldn't find one. During a vacation I found a shop in Paris that stocked them. I lugged three of them home.

To lubricate the overhead valve gear, the rocker shaft, and the rockers it was necessary to remove the valve cover and anoint the rocker shaft by pouring on a mixture of oil and kerosene. The clutch bearing was lubricated archaically, by means of a brush dipped in grease. You first had to lift a floorboard and then remove the clutch cover.

One of the more traumatic troubles I had with the RLSS was due to my own ignorance. My brother and I had been driving down the elevated West Side Highway in New York City. That roadway was fairly rough even forty-odd years ago. After negotiating a bump we heard a God-awful bang from underneath the car. When we got home I got under the car to investigate. According to a picture in the instruction book, which I had recently acquired and which I had devoured, the torque member that ran alongside the drive shaft was missing. I was devastated. We rushed back to the elevated highway to look for it. It was not there. We looked under the roadway. Not there either.

Top: 1908 Darracq-built ancestor of the Alfa Romeo.
Bottom: Author's 1925 RLSS 3-liter Alfa Romeo touring car,
photographed in 1934. The engine of this Super
Sport version of the RL model developed 83 hp at 3,600 rpm.
The author reached 87 mph—once. Bumpers were installed
to cope with New York City parking habits.

*1,500-cc Alfa Romeos racing in Ireland in 1929.
Starting in the late 1920's, comparatively small 1,500-cc
and 1,750-cc Alfa Romeos competed against
gargantuan machines like the 4$^1/_2$-liter Bentleys and
38/250 Mercedes-Benzes and, as often as not,
showed the big brutes their dust.*

We asked people. We stopped a garbage truck. The sanitation men were wildly excited about seeing an Italian car, but they hadn't seen such-and-such a piece of metal. I was about to cable Milan to order a new torque arm, when the ex-owner of the Alfa told me that only the normal RL model had such an arm, that despite the anchorages on the differential casing and a chassis cross-member, the RLSS had no such torque arm. We never did find out what caused that bang.

Despite the fact that the Alfa was unbearably hot to drive in summer, due in part to its aluminum toe board becoming almost molten, I loved that wonderful old machine. In the early thirties no car I knew except a 3-liter Bentley owned by a friend was in the same class with it. It had wonderfully quick steering and fantastic roadholding compared with American cars. And it made a most wonderful hair-raising bellow when its exhaust cutout was open and the exhaust gases emerged through a sort of bronze megaphone. Italians have always loved the loud music some cars could make.

I had been attracted to the RLSS Alfa Romeo largely because of what I'd read about the exploits of Grand Prix Alfas in the British motoring press—*The Autocar, The Motor, Motor Sport*. Alfa had tried to start Grand Prix racing with its Merosi-designed P1 in 1923. Three were built. But Alfa's best-loved driver, Ugo Sivocci, practicing for the Italian Grand Prix at Monza in a P1, lost control on a curve and crashed fatally. Alfa withdrew the other P1's for good. Never again were they entered in a race.

The P1 was succeeded by the P2. And the P2 that, driven by Giuseppe Campari, won the first important Grand Prix for which it was entered—the Grand Prix of Europe at Lyons in August, 1924—was designed by a new man at Alfa Romeo, the great Vittorio Jano, who would make Alfa Romeo *the* name among sports and racing cars for many years to come. Jano had been at Fiat but was wooed away with promises of more money and a free hand.

The P2 Alfa Romeo was similar to the racing machines Jano had designed for Fiat. It had a 2-liter straight-eight engine with twin overhead camshafts. And it was supercharged by means of a Roots-type blower. There wasn't much in this design that was really radical. Twin-ohc racing engines had been designed by Ernest Henry as far back as 1912 for the then-revolutionary Grand Prix Peugeot.

The P2's did brilliantly, and in 1925 Alfa Romeo became the world's champions. The new formula for Grand Prix cars in 1926 was to be 1½ liters. Alfa decided that the expense of developing a new Grand Prix machine was too much. In any case, the time had come to bring out new designs for sports and touring cars to replace the RL and RLSS models. So Alfa quit Grand Prix racing while it was ahead. The sports cars, however, still raced.

The new cars would embrace what had been learned in racing and also take full advantage of Jano's very superior skills. Some

of the loveliest sporting cars of all time were in the wings.

But the first of the new line of cars first shown at the Milan Automobile Show in the spring of 1925 was not a sports car but the rather less muscular 6C 1500 Turismo model. And no one could buy it until 1927. The new small Alfa had a six-cylinder, 1,487-cc engine with a single overhead camshaft driven by bevel gears from a vertical shaft at the rear of the engine. Construction and finish were impeccable. The counterbalanced crankshaft, for example, was machined and polished all over and ran on five main bearings. The nondetachable-headed block was a masterpiece of foundry work. (Italians have always been superb foundrymen.) Ignition was by coil, and the distributor was driven off the vertical drive for the camshaft. The unique valve-adjustment method was the same as that which would be used on all descendants of this first Jano-designed passenger car until the 1950's. It delighted me years later when I owned subsequent models. Attached to the top of each valve stem were two toothed discs, the upper one being the tappet against which the cam bore. A special tool was supplied with two small, toothed segments, one movable, the other stationary. The tool was first fitted into a socket cast into the head. The tool's lower toothed segment prevented the lower disc on the valve from turning. The upper toothed segment turned the upper disc to adjust the valve clearance. Simple and neat! But we do not know if Jano actually invented it. The Hispano-Suiza already used a similar if slightly less sophisticated system. Only 44 bhp was developed.

The chassis was a simple ladder frame with semielliptic springs. The four-speed gearbox transmitted power through a torque tube. Top speed was not much over 65 mph.

It wasn't long before customers demanded a more sporting machine from Alfa Romeo. Hadn't they recently been champions of the world? So in 1928 a 6C 1500 Sport was announced. The engine was different from that in the Turismo. It now had a detachable head with twin overhead camshafts and hemispherical combustion chambers, larger valves, and higher compression. Now, with light open sports coachwork, over 75 mph was possible, for the engine developed 54 bhp.

The next step was the Super Sport model, with a shorter chassis and lighter body. The engine had its compression ratio raised again and now produced 60 bhp. A supercharged version of the Super Sport with its Roots-type blower driven from the front of the crankshaft was offered in 1929. To make room for the blower the engine was moved rearward 15 inches. Another version of the Super Sport had its engine moved back but was *"senza compressore"* (without blower). With the blower the Super Sport now developed 76 bhp and was capable of close to 90 mph. But Jano would do better. In 1929 the first 1750 was shown at the Rome Auto Show. There was of course a cooking version, the 1750 Turismo. But it was the 6C 1750 Super Sport and Gran Sport versions,

Top: 1919 poster advertising Alfa Romeos.
Bottom: Sir Henry Birkin and Tazio Nuvolari with a
2.3-liter supercharged Alfa Romeo at the Ulster
T.T. race in 1931. Nuvolari wears the famous yellow
jerkin without which he seldom sat
behind the wheel of a racing car.

The 1929 6C 1750 Super Sport *senza compressore*
(unblown) Alfa Romeo had a six-cylinder twin-overhead-camshaft
engine that was set as far back in the frame as that
of the supercharged model. This car, owned by the author from
1936 to 1939, was capable of over 85 mph. Driving
light and bumpers were strictly nonstandard.

in my view among the greatest sports cars ever built, that excited sports-car connoisseurs everywhere. If there ever existed the near-perfect sports car, the 1750 Gran Sport Alfa was it.

In 1936 I still owned my RLSS 3-liter Alfa. I loved it dearly, but I'd had a problem with it. The radiator, beautifully constructed of square sectioned tubing and pointed à la Mercedes, was corroded and somewhat constipated. Nowadays knowledgeable restorers would almost certainly find a way to revitalize such a nice piece of work. But in the early 1930's I followed the advice of the people at Zumbach's. The radiator was scrapped and a modern, flat, American radiator was substituted. The pointed upper and lower tanks were retained and the open maw between them was filled with pieces of Cadillac grille that had a square section pattern not unlike that of the original radiator. (You can see the Cadillac grillwork in the accompanying photograph.)

Soon after the operation I heard of a sports two-seater Alfa Romeo for sale. I didn't know one model Alfa from another; I'm sure no one else in America did, either, in those days. Later I found that it was a 1,750-cc Super Sport *senza compressore*, complete with twin overhead camshafts.

The Alfa lay in a garage in Greenwich Village in New York. Mechanically it seemed perfect, save for a lack of shock absorbers which its owner, Giuseppe Fantacci, had removed in a misguided effort to spare his girl friend's bottom from road shocks. Its elegant

sports two-seater body (there was no maker's name on it) was in fair shape except for a few dings and dents. But it was painted a hideously dull shade of gray and was somewhat weather-worn. I was entranced by the lovely-looking little machine. From its slanted nickeled radiator to its tightly tucked-in tail it looked exactly like my dream of a sports car. The engine, with its twin dull-finished aluminum camshaft covers and its clean, uncluttered, sculptured look, amazed me. Except for the engine under the hood of my RLSS Alfa, I'd been used to the greasy iron of American cars. But even the RLSS engine didn't look like a work of art. This one did. I couldn't wait to give the man the money—all $700.

Zumbach's found little to do with the mechanics of the car. They did put in new spark plugs and new plug wires. New Hartford shockers were installed. Then they sent it to a body shop for new paint and a bit of plating here and there. When I came to collect the Alfa I was astounded at the change Zumbach's had wrought. The Alfa looked and sounded like new. But before I could get my hands on the wheel and my feet on the pedals, Fantacci and my brother vaulted into the car and screamed off in it, with Fantacci driving. Half an hour later, after a foray into New York City traffic, they returned—my brother shaken, Fantacci delirious with praise for his old car. When I finally got to drive it, I was delirious, too. For never had I driven anything the like of it. The Alfa's almost too instant response to the throttle,

its superbly quick and accurate steering, its incredible roadholding, were beyond anything in my previous experience.

We've been led to believe that our ongoing excitement over sports cars is largely due to drivers first tasting the pleasures of the MG soon after World War II. Not true. When, in 1936, I advertised my 22/90 RLSS Alfa Romeo in the Sunday New York *Times*, I got forty calls within a few days. The first guy phoned while I was still abed that Sunday morning. He got the Alfa. I still regret selling it.

That first 1750 Super Sport (*senza compressore*) Alfa was, of course, superb. But some years later I became the joyful owner of an even better one. This was a 1750 super-charged Gran Sport. A late fifth-series Zagato-bodied model, No. 10816391, built in 1933.

This blown Alfa was, of course, faster than my old unblown Super Sport. Top speed was near 100 mph. Zero to 60 took about eleven seconds. The engine was even more willing. I had to be careful not to accidentally step on the gas pedal (which lived *between* the clutch and brake pedals) when getting out of the car with the engine running, lest revs instantly scream up past the red line, which was 4,500 rpm.

The steering was much as I remembered from the unblown Super Sport, but I always had the feeling that the Gran Sport's was not quite so good, perhaps because the added weight of the supercharger up front slightly changed the balance of the machine. It's true,

1933 SC 2600 supercharged Mille Miglia Alfa Romeo.
Its twin-overhead-camshaft engine developed some 185 hp
and was said to be capable of some 125 mph.
This is the famous ex-Templar car that ran in the
"Fastest Sports Car" race at Brooklands in
1939. A sports Delahaye won.

what has been said of 1750 steering. You did not steer consciously. The signal from your brain to your hands seemed to do the steering. But try consciously to hold a straight course while tightly gripping the wheel and you'd *not* hold a straight course. A 1750 knew the way.

It must be remembered that 1750's had leaf springs all around. On a fast bumpy corner there was a bit of hopping. But the machine was so agile, so well balanced, and so quick to answer the helm that an accurate course around a rutted bumpy corner could be held without any fancy steering.

The Gran Sport 1750 had its little foibles. The spare oil tank at the left side of the cockpit seemed sometimes to weep oil, with untoward affects on trousers or silk stockings (they were worn in the thirties). The instrument panel was almost hidden under the cowl. The rev counter was visible enough. But bend to read the oil-pressure gauge and you blew the horn with your chin. To vary toe-in of the front wheels it was necessary to brutally bend the track rod. There was no other adjustment. At least I couldn't figure any other way to do it.

If there was one sin the 1750 driver had to guard against, it was a savage attitude toward the small multiple-disc clutch. Slip the clutch when trying to get out of sand or snow and the steel plates overheated and distorted. Once, trying to extricate myself from sand near Montauk Point, Long Island, I thus murdered the clutch, which locked itself solid. I had to drive the 120 miles to New York clutchlessly.

A 1750 was by no means a fussy machine to maintain. A little oil was mixed with the gasoline to help lubricate the supercharger. On late models there was also a grease fitting. Earlier models required that the blower's front plate be removed to allow Vaseline to be smeared on the bearings.

Starting in winter, even if the 1750 hadn't run for weeks, was never an onerous exercise. It merely required that the rather crude Memini carburetor be tickled to flood the float chamber. And this reminds me that my Gran Sport 1750 was not too economical of fuel: 9 miles per gallon when the car was driven with verve. And a blown 1750 was *always* driven with verve. When accelerating hard from a standstill a sphere of black smoke emerged flatulently from the tailpipe.

How do you tell a blown Gran Sport from a Super Sport? The carburetor of a Super Sport is on the right side of the supercharger and the offtake from the blower crosses over the top of it. The Gran Sport carburetor is on the left of the supercharger and no crossover is needed. Further, the finned intake manifold of the Gran Sport is more complex than the Super Sport's. It is perhaps the most beautiful casting ever made for an engine.

From the very beginning, when the twin-ohc sports version of the 6C 1500 first appeared in 1929, enthusiastic customers entered races and hill climbs, doing very well, indeed. So the Alfa factory soon had second thoughts about its 1925 decision to forgo racing. In 1927

Top: 1938 8C 2900B Alfa Romeo. The four-passenger coupe body is by Touring of Milan. Closed coachwork was mounted on the Lungo *(long) chassis.*
Bottom: Beautifully finished supercharged eight-cylinder twin-overhead-camshaft 8C 2900B engine developed 180 hp at 5,200 rpm.

Enzo Ferrari and Attilio Marinoni took a couple of unblown twin-cam Super Sport 1500's to the Circuit of Modena and took first and second spots.

In 1928 Campari won the Mille Miglia, in a special fixed-head supercharged 1500 Super Sport. In 1929 Campari and Giulio Ramponi again won the Mille Miglia, but this time with blown 1750's with fixed heads and bigger-than-standard valves that gave them 95 bhp and 103 mph.

In 1930 Mercedes-Benz entered the Mille Miglia with two of its monstrous 7-liter blown SSK sports cars driven by Caracciola and Wagner. With 225 bhp and a top speed of 125 mph, they should have been invincible. But Alfa Romeo had the great Tazio Nuvolari in the cockpit of one of its blown 1750's. Driving another 1750 was Achille Varzi, Nuvolari's sworn rival. The race developed into a duel between the two teammates that Alfa's racing manager, Enzo Ferrari, tried to cool down. He signaled Varzi that Nuvolari had slowed and was in a hopeless position. Nuvolari caught Varzi by sneaking up on him at night with his lights out. Nuvolari won. The best one of the trucklike Mercedes driven by "Carratsch" could manage was sixth place, with four of the more nimble 1750 Alfas ahead of it.

In 1929 Enzo Ferrari ostensibly left Alfa Romeo, where he had so successfully campaigned the 1500's and 1750's, and set up the Scuderia Ferrari in Modena. He was to be an Alfa Romeo dealer, but his chief concern was the management of Alfa's racing efforts. More powerful cars would be needed to make those efforts successful.

In 1931 Vittorio Jano came up with the 8C 2300. Its 2,336-cc straight-eight engine, like that of the 1750, had twin overhead camshafts and hemispherical combustion chambers. The cylinders consisted of two four-cylinder blocks end to end. The crankshaft, too, was split in the middle, with a pair of gears between the two halves. These gears drove the camshafts, the supercharger that sat on the right side of the engine and the water and oil pumps, and also the generator. The superbly finished and balanced crankshaft ran on no fewer than ten main bearings. The blower produced 6 pounds of pressure. Although the compression ratio was only 5.75 to 1, a lively 144 bhp was developed at 5,000 rpm.

The chassis frame was of a simple ladder type and tended to flex on rough roads. The light, simple, businesslike bodywork by Zagato and Castagna suffered a bit from the chassis' lack of rigidity, and it was rather shaking to watch the doors moving longitudinally relative to the bodywork. Leaf springs held almost immovably rigid by Hartford-type shock absorbers contributed to a hard ride. But there was a wonderful tight springiness about the suspension that made that hard ride rather pleasurable. The chassis came in two lengths: the *Corto* (short), with a 108-inch wheelbase, and the *Lungo* (long), with no less than a 124-inch wheelbase. The slightly lighter *Corto* weighed only about 2,500 pounds and was capable of over 110

Top: 1932 Zagato-bodied 1,750-cc supercharged Gran Sport Alfa Romeo. Middle: Tazio Nuvolari drives twelve-cylinder Grand Prix Alfa Romeo at Roosevelt Raceway, New York, in 1937. Bottom: 1938 version of the Type 158 1,500-cc Grand Prix car. By 1951 the 195-hp 158 had been developed into the 425-hp Type 159.

mph; the *Lungo*, some 200 pounds heavier, was scarcely slower. Huge wheel-filling ribbed brakes did a remarkable job of retardation for the time.

I've driven 2.3 Alfas fairly often. They're superb machines—brutal, with suitably nervous steering, and very quick indeed. But when it comes to handling, I'll take a 1750. Perhaps the heavier engine of the 8C 2300 makes it just a wee bit less charming than a 1750.

The Depression was no time to sell very expensive sports cars. An 8C 2300 cost some $10,000 in 1932—about equal to the cost of a Ferrari Boxer in today's degraded currency. Fewer than two hundred were sold.

Alfa Romeo might have gone bust in the early thirties had Mussolini not come to the rescue. He needed Alfa Romeo to help him trumpet the glories of *fascismo*. His Istituto Recostruzione Industriale poured lire into the faltering company, which thenceforth was government controlled. It still is.

Alfa then repaid Il Duce by going out and winning races with special racing versions of the 2.3. Until Hitler's Mercedes-Benzes and Auto-Unions took the field Alfa Romeo reigned supreme. The Bugattis that had dominated Grand Prix racing for years were now outclassed.

Amazingly, the new Grand Prix Alfas were derived from sports cars instead of the other way round. In 1931 at the European Grand Prix at Monza near Milan, Campari won over two 4.9-liter and two 2.3-liter Bugattis in a 2.3 Alfa that had been shortened, lightened, and given a pointed tail and a slightly modified engine that put out 178 bhp. After this first outing as a Grand Prix car, the 2,300-cc Alfa was named the Monza. The Monzas did very well, but Jano was not satisfied.

After a flirtation with a twelve-cylinder Grand Prix car, the Tipo A, which had two blown 1,750-cc engines side by side under the hood plus two clutches and gearboxes, Jano produced his greatest racing machine, the Monoposto Tipo B—the famous P3.

The engine was based on that in the Monza, which had been derived from the 8C 2300 sports car. But it was slightly larger—2,654 cc—and it had bigger valves, too. Twin superchargers, each feeding one of the four-cylinder blocks, replaced the earlier single blower. Brake horsepower was 215, and later P3's developed as much as 255 bhp. The drive to the rear wheels was divided. From the differential, which was now amidships next to the transmission, two drive shafts in V-formation each drove a rear wheel. This not only allowed the driver of the single-seat P3 to sit lower, it reduced unsprung weight in the rear and dramatically improved the roadholding of the still archaically leaf-sprung chassis. Even early models were capable of 143 mph.

It was in the Italian Grand Prix at Monza, in 1932, that the P3 first showed its stuff. Nuvolari on a P3 came in first, Borzacchini on a Monza was third, and another P3 driven by Campari came in fourth. The rest of the season was one triumph after another. In spite of this, because of obscure fiscal problems, the P3's were withdrawn for 1933. The Scuderia Ferrari had to mount its drivers on Monzas instead of P3's. The Monzas, bored out to 2.6 liters, did fairly well, but the P3's would have done much better.

In July of 1933, the Alfa factory, cognizant of the deficiencies of the Monza as compared with the P3, changed its mind and once more gave the Scuderia Ferrari P3's. For 1934 the P3's engines were bored out to 2.9 liters. Compression was raised and the supercharger pressure increased. They now got 163 mph from 255 bhp. Later, one with a more modern aerodynamic body would reach 175 mph.

But Alfa's great racing years were coming to an end. The new German Auto-Unions and Mercedes-Benzes saw to that. Even with independent suspensions and hydraulic brakes, the 8C 35 model, the V-twelve-cylinder 12C 36 and 12C 37 models, and the sixteen-cylinder Tipo 316 model Alfa Romeo won few Grand Prix races in the years just before World War II. To keep Alfa's name alive the small 1½-liter Tipo 158 Alfetta designed by Gioacchino Colombo was brought out to compete in *voiturette* racing. The Alfettas, happily, did very well indeed under the aegis of Alfa-Corse, which now managed Alfa Romeo's racing. That is, until the Germans showed up with 1½-liter Mercedes V-8's at the Tripoli Grand Prix in 1939.

Even as the war started, new racing machines, including the Tipo 512, a rear-en-gined abomination similar to the successful Auto-Unions, were on the stocks. But the war soon put an end to such whistling in the dark.

During the 1930's Alfa Romeo built not only sports cars and racing cars but also bread-and-butter machines for rich Italians who enjoyed showing the Great Name emblazoned on their family sedans. They expected that such cars would have all the attributes of sports and racing Alfas. So such cars as the 6C 1900 and the 6C 2300 Turismo, Pescara, and Gran Turismo models were turned out. But, contrary to their owners' expectations, most of these dull cars offered no great power or speed. The 6C 2300 Turismo of 1934 had but 68 bhp and a top speed of 75 mph. At the top of the scale, however, the 6C 2300B Pescara with 95 bhp could be pushed to 90 mph.

In spite of their modest performance, these cooking Alfas by no means resembled the ironmongery Detroit was turning out, for their engines had twin overhead camshafts, hemispherical heads, and seven-bearing crankshafts. Not all had standard stamped-out steel bodies. Some were offered with luxurious if heavy bodies by *carrossiers* like Castagna. Nor did these cars handle like mass-produced Detroit machinery. For they were indeed Alfas, with accurate steering and nimble road manners. Still, sporting Italians in love with the earlier 1750 Gran Sport and 8C 2300 open two-seaters tended to take a jaundiced view of such comfortable touring cars, some of which to their dis-

8C 2900B Alfa Romeo with "Superleggera" body
by Touring of Milan. In 1938 this car cost $11,000
in New York. Purists were critical of the lush
bodywork, which they compared with the design of the
vulgar Auburn Speedster. Alfas, they felt,
should be lean and stark.

dain had synchromesh gearboxes and independent front suspension.

From 1937 until Mussolini dragged Italy into World War II, Alfa Romeo built the most powerful sports car a private owner could buy in those days. This was the 8C 2900B, which Jano based on the thirty-odd Monoposto engines left over when the Grand Prix cars were fitted with V-12's.

A friend of mine ordered such an 8C 2900B in 1938 but had a terrible time getting delivery. In the end he journeyed to Milan and sat on Alfa Romeo's doorstep until he was able to pry his new car out of them. When it was removed from its crate in front of Zumbach's, I was one of the hangers-on ooh-ing and ah-ing over the svelte red *"Superleggera"* coachwork by Touring of Milan. But the 2.9 didn't look like the kind of Alfa I'd been used to. It looked too fat, too slick, and, dare I say it, too much like an Auburn Speedster.

It certainly did look like a proper Alfa under the hood, though. There lay the straight-eight, twin-overhead-camshaft engine with its twin blowers and its beautifully cast finned intake manifolds. Further, the engine made all the right delicious noises we'd learned to expect from the old 8C 2300 Alfa Romeos, And it wasn't merely noise that the beautiful engine made—it developed a lusty 180 bhp at 5,000 rpm. A top speed of 115 mph was possible. Zero to 60 mph took nine seconds. Independent suspension was used both front and rear. This required an inflexible chassis frame, which was achieved by building it of stiff box-section members. Brakes were hydraulic. The clutch was up near the engine, but the gearbox lay aft.

The owner of the 2.9 took me for a ride once in return for a ride I'd given him in my 1750, which he said had prompted him to buy his car. We didn't go very fast that day on our run through New York's Central Park. Perhaps if we had I'd have liked the car better. First, I felt too enveloped by the superstreamlined body. We sat too low in the thing. I was used to sitting *on* not *in*, my Alfas. Further, the machine hadn't that nervous stiffness I thought an Alfa ought to have. It felt soft.

How much did such a luxurious Alfa Romeo cost in 1938? $11,000. Considering inflation, about as much as a Ferrari costs today.

After the war, not too much was left of the Alfa Romeo factories. But somehow, by the end of 1946, six-cylinder 2500's in both Sport and Turismo versions became available. These were originally developed from the old 6C 2300B machines of prewar days.

Previously, no dealers had imported Alfas into the United States, but with the post-war interest in foreign cars a few 6C 2500's came in. People who'd been familiar with sporting prewar examples tended to sneer at these Alfa sedans. But the 6C 2500's were not all that bad. The Turismo model, with 87 bhp, was capable of almost 90 mph. The Sport, with 95 bhp and a lighter body, was about 5 mph faster. A Super Sport version, which never came into this coun-

Three aspects of the 1962 Giulia Spider Veloce roadster. Four-cylinder, 1,570-cc, twin-overhead-camshaft engine gave it a speed of 105 mph. The Giulia was a development of the earlier Giulietta, which had a slightly smaller 1,300-cc engine. Both machines were delightful to drive, albeit a bit fragile.

*Above: 1947 6C 2500 Sport Alfa Romeo with
convertible body by Farina. Its twin-overhead-camshaft
engine developed some 95 hp. Top speed was
about 95 mph. Top right: 1973 Alfa Romeo Montreal had
a 230-hp V-8 engine. Bottom right: Alfa Corse
advertisement for a race in Tripoli.*

try, was much lighter and could reach 105 mph.

The first really new postwar Alfa Romeo was the four-cylinder Berlina 1900, which made its debut in 1950. It is from this excellent little machine that most Alfas up to the present are descended. And it was the 1900 that first brought the company into the big world of mass production.

Its twin-overhead-camshaft, hemispherical combustion-chambered engine with a moderate 7½-to-1 compression and one carburetor developed 90 bhp and propelled the sveltely contoured 1900 at almost 95 mph, for chassisless monocoque construction kept its weight down to 2,500 pounds. It was the first Alfa Romeo to abandon right-hand drive, which had been retained in supersports cars (including the Bugatti) even in countries with a right-hand rule of the

road. An unlikable feature of the 1900 was its steering-column gear change.

Incredibly, Alfa was more successful in Grand Prix racing in the early postwar years than it had been before the war. And the winning cars were the 1½-liter Alfettas—the old 158's first built for *voiturette* racing back in 1938. They had, of course, been continually improved and by 1946 twin superchargers had been fitted. In 1951, when the 158's had been further revised and improved, they became known as 159's. Horsepower had been a mere 195 at 7,200 rpm in 1938, but by 1951 power had risen to 425 bhp at 9,300 rpm. To go on winning Grands Prix after 1951 it would have been necessary for Alfa Romeo to invest many millions of lire in the development of new racing machines. But Alfa was a different kind of company by 1951. It was more important to concentrate on mass production than on racing. So Alfa quit Grand Prix racing but still continued to enter lesser forms of competition, first with hot versions of the 1900 and then with various examples of the super-streamlined Disco Volante—literally, "flying saucer"—which was at first fitted with a 1900 engine.

Before the 1900 went out of production more puissant models were brought out: the Super, the TI, the TI Super, the Sprint, and the Super Sprint. Some of these had as much as 115 bhp and could reach 106 mph.

But there was an even better machine on the stocks—the Giulietta, which appeared in 1954. There was a whole gaggle of Giulietta models, from the sedate Berlina to the Bertone Sprint Speciale, which had a 100-bhp engine and a top speed of 124 mph. The one I owned was an open two-seater designed by Pininfarina, the Giulietta Spider Veloce, as pleasing a little machine as I've ever driven.

The Spider Veloce was fitted with a four-cylinder, 1,290-cc engine with twin chain-driven overhead camshafts and a twin-choke carburetor. Its notably clean and good-looking engine looked little different from today's Alfa engines. It had an aluminum block with cast-iron cylinder liners and a five-bearing crankshaft. With an 8½-to-1 compression ratio it put out 90 bhp, enough to push the 1,936-pound car along at over 105 mph. A four-speed gearbox with a floor change and Porsche-type synchromesh made gear-changing a pleasure despite a tendency to wear out the synchromesh cones. Front suspension was by wishbones and coil spring. The rear axle was rigid and also suspended by coil springs.

Surprisingly, this Giulietta had much of the feel of its ancestor, the Gran Sport 1750 that I had owned so many years earlier. It had the same nimbleness, the same taut, light steering, even some of the same sounds. Although faster it felt slower, and it had none of the old hard, exciting nervousness. Nor was its admittedly pretty engine in the same class as the spectacularly beautiful 1750's. Further, the valves of the Giulietta were adjusted by means of shims. The toothed valve tappets of the 1750 were too expensive for mass production.

I had my troubles with the Giulietta. Most modern Alfa Romeo agents' repair departments are little better than those of the unknowledgeable and rapacious dealers of American cars. Once when I took the Giulietta in for valve adjustment, the mechanics sent me out without water in the radiator. I first noticed the lack in the middle of a crowded bridge. By the time I could stop, the cylinder head was irretrievably warped. I had universal joint troubles, too. Other Giuliettas I knew of had frightful rust problems. One, a rather ancient example owned by my son, had its body-cum-chassis so rust-eaten as to sag amidships. Its engine lived on in another Alfa.

The 1,300-cc Giulietta in its many guises was enlarged into various 1,600-cc Giulias starting in 1962 but not before Alfa brought out an enlarged 1900—the 2000, which was produced both as a Berlina and a Spider. The Spider, with a 115-bhp engine, was capable of 115 mph. Somehow the 2000 and the later six-cylinder 2600, which appeared in 1962, had not the charm of either the Giulietta or the Giulia. I only drove a 2600 once. Although it was fast (124 mph), had plenty of power (145 bhp), and had luxurious bodywork, I felt it was rather a lump compared with a Giulietta.

At about this time Alfa Romeo built a gruesome little mistake sponsored by the Italian motoring magazine *Quattroruote*. This was an imitation Gran Sport 1750 with a Zagato body. Its proportions were hideous: its radiator was too far forward, its cockpit too big. It was fast, since it used a Giulia engine, but it looked no more like a 1750 Gran Sport than an Excalibur looks like an SSK Mercedes-Benz.

That old 1,300-cc Giulietta engine keeps on growing. First it went to 1,600 cc, then to 1,750 cc, and now it lives on in the 2,000-cc-engined Sprint Veloce and in the lovely 2000 Spider Veloce. The Sprint Veloce with fuel injection, rear-mounted five-speed gearbox, and De Dion rear axle is as fine a 2 + 2 sports sedan as anyone could wish for. The Spider is the car to buy if open-air motoring is your thing. But I'll be quite surprised if this last of the open Alfas is still in production by the time you read these words.

There was a bigger-engined Alfa Romeo for a while in recent years: the V-8 2,593-cc-engined Montreal, which put out 230 bhp at 6,500 rpm. This 135-mph GT coupe, which first appeared at the Montreal Expo 67, was not marketed in the United States because it couldn't meet Federal requirements. I did, however, get a ride in one that slipped in from Canada. I was much excited by it, despite the fact that the driver couldn't really unleash it in the crowded suburb where he demonstrated it. It showed its racing background, for it was after all descended from the fairly successful T/33 sports racing machines that Autodelta, the Alfa-backed racing organization, campaigned. But at over $25,000 per copy it would not have sold too well in the United States.

Alfa Romeo builds another machine that, at this writing, is not yet sold in the United

States. This, the Alfasud, is built near Naples. Alfa is, after all, government-run, and it was the government's view that one way to put unemployed south Italians to work was to set them to building small, low-priced Alfa Romeos. The result is a fine little car indeed. It has a flat four 1,186-cc, 63-bhp engine that drives the front wheels, and a beautifully designed compact body by Giugiario. A surprising 93 mph is realized. A hotter version, the Alfasud T1, offers 68 bhp and 100 mph. Spoilers front and rear help keep the little fellow on the road.

I'm looking forward, too, to driving the new Giulietta. Thus far only the wedge-profiled sedan has been shown, but can a Spider be far behind? The excellent old twin-cam engine

*1978 Alfa Romeo Sprint Veloce GTV has a
2,000-cc fuel-injected four-cylinder engine, and
a five-speed gearbox mounted in the rear in
conjunction with a De Dion rear axle. The excellent
engine is a grown-up version of the one the factory
has used for a quarter-century or more.*

is available in both 1,300-cc and 1,600-cc sizes in Italy, but it seems that only the 1,600-cc version will be sold in this country. The 1600 develops 109 bhp. As in its bigger sister, the Sprint Veloce sports sedan, the gearbox lives with the De Dion rear axle. A friend of mine drove one through the mountains of Sicily recently. He says it's even better on corners than the first Giulietta. But it will cost twice as much—about $8,000.

Which of all the Alfa Romeos built since 1910 would I like to have? I'd like my old blown 1750 Gran Sport back again. But the hard man who owns it is talking about $50,000. That's what I get for talking all these years about how wonderful Alfa Romeos are.

Duesenberg

The Duesenberg is *the* gilt-edged investment for the motorcar collector who cares less about cars than about owning an appreciating asset that, he thinks, also gives him a certain prestige. There are, I fear, some of these gentry who would happily store their Duesenbergs in safe-deposit boxes if such repositories could be made big enough. For they almost never drive their huge possessions. They transport them in weathertight trailers from meet to meet in order to garner prizes that increase the market value of their once-mobile cars.

The J, SJ, and SSJ Duesenbergs that were built between 1928 and 1937 are the machines most coveted and cosseted by that special breed of Duesenberg fanciers, but the marque Duesenberg was initiated long before the overblown J appeared.

The Duesenberg brothers, Frederick Samuel and his younger brother, August, were brought from Germany to America as babies and grew up on a farm near Rockford, Iowa. Fred was of a mechanical bent and at seventeen got a job with a dealer in farm machinery for whom he helped repair plows and combines and such. He also assisted in erecting windmills used for pumping water. In 1897, when the bicycle craze was in full bloom, he became involved with building and repairing the early "safety" bicycles. Like so many other young men who later got into automobiles, he started racing bicycles, then motorcycles, and inevitably became interested in horseless carriages.

Soon he was working for Thomas Jeffery, who was building a horseless called the Rambler in Kenosha, Wisconsin. He stayed with Rambler for a few years as a tester and then opened his own garage in Des Moines, Iowa—the Iowa Automobile and Supply Company. But Fred had larger ambitions. He had his own ideas about what a motorcar should be and how it ought to be designed and built. His chief interest was speed.

Nowadays any young man looking toward a career in the design of automobiles gets himself a degree in engineering. Fred Duesenberg was barely literate. But a Des Moines lawyer named Mason, who was interested in getting into the new business of automobiles, told him to go ahead, he'd back him with money. The two-cylinder Mason—"The Fastest and Strongest 2-cylinder Car in America"—built by the Mason Motor Car Company was the result. The Mason car was quite successful and did well in minor racing, which was then an important means of advertising. The Mason Company became the Maytag-Mason Motor Company when it was bought by F. L. Maytag in 1910.

In 1913 two Masons built by the Duesenbergs ran in the Indianapolis 500. One of them, driven by Jack Tower, was the fastest qualifier at 88.23 mph. It finished nineteenth. The other, driven by the famous Willie Haupt, finished fifteenth. Encouraged, the brothers

Preceding pages: 1931 Model J Duesenberg
with convertible roadster body by Murphy of Pasadena,
California. This unsupercharged version, which
had a twin-overhead-camshaft 7-liter engine,
was claimed to reach no less than 116 mph from the
265 hp the engine was said to develop.

formed the Duesenberg Motor company in St. Paul, Minnesota. There they built race cars and engines, including a marine engine for the first boat to do better than a mile a minute.

During World War I the Duesenbergs, by then in Elizabeth, New Jersey, became involved with building a sixteen-cylinder, 500-hp airplane engine designed by the quixotic Italian genius Ettore Bugatti. This engine was, in effect, two straight eights geared to each other side by side. Later there were murmurings that the straight-eight Duesenberg engines that appeared after the war owed something to Monsieur Bugatti's designs. (Bugatti didn't build a straight-eight car engine until 1923.) It was such a straight eight that powered the Duesenberg car in which Jimmy Murphy won the 1921 French Grand Prix at Le Mans. (Not the later twenty-four-hour race.) No American had done it before, and the French were delighted with the young American driver. (The French still tolerated Americans in those post-World War I days.) And they were much intrigued by the sophisticated 3-liter overhead-camshaft engine and the four-wheel hydraulic brakes first used by Duesenberg. The steel brake shoes were actuated by cylinders that were machined out of blocks of marine bronze. The master cylinder was hinged to the chassis and moved as the brake pedal was depressed; the piston stood still. The brake fluid was water with a little glycerine added to prevent freezing. The water ran through a hollow front axle and kingpins to the wheel cylinders.

Only 115 bhp was developed by the engine, but it was enough to propel the 1,750-pound Duesenberg at an average speed of 78.2 mph—fast for that rough and stony course. Toward the end a stone through the radiator emptied it of coolant, but the red-hot engine kept running. Further, Murphy's 83.2-mph lap record was not beaten until 1929.

By the mid-1920's the Duesenberg was one of the stars of the Indianapolis 500, winning in 1924, 1925, and 1927. By then, too, the Duesenberg brothers' factory had been moved to Indianapolis.

In October, 1920, the first Duesenberg passenger car, the Model A, was shown at the Automobile Salon in New York. The A incorporated many of the features that had been used in the Duesenberg racing machines: liberal use of light alloys, hydraulic brakes, and a straight-eight engine. Although mechanically advanced for 1920, the styling of the bodies was prosaic. Despite its low price—considering its high quality—the Model A didn't sell very well, and Duesenberg Motors went into receivership in 1926.

A sharp, wheeler-dealer salesman type, Erret Lobban Cord, seized control. He had been highly successful at selling the cheap Auburn by restyling it, and he killed off the Model A in favor of making that smallish pedestrian machine into a giant and flamboyant supercar. When Cord acquired Duesenberg he also took control of Lycoming Motors of Williamsport, Pennsylvania, a company engaged in

building engines for manufacturers of assembled cars. Fred Duesenberg became Engineering Vice President, his brother August got the title of Assistant Chief Engineer.

The J Duesenberg was built for the very rich. And there were enough of them around in the palmy days of the late twenties to pay $14,000 for a fancy automobile. Even after the stock-market crash of 1929 and the Great Depression that followed, there still were people with enough money to buy Duesenbergs for almost a decade. If you're really loaded, depressions don't bother you much.

Advertisements in magazines like *Vanity Fair* and *Town & Country* showed purportedly ultrarich types in their baronial pads,

The svelte, European-looking, convertible cabriolet
body on the 1929 Model J Duesenberg is by the famed carrossier
Graber of Switzerland, who succeeded in making the
car look less massive than those with bodies by American
coachbuilders. The hood looks narrower than usual, but the
magnificent engine nestles neatly within it.

their yachts, their bigger-than-Versailles gardens. The single line of copy said, "He drives a Duesenberg." With advertising like that, and with a fellow like E. L. Cord in charge, you might expect that the Duesenberg would be a somewhat spurious car. It wasn't. The Duesenberg was a splendid car, indeed, perhaps the best car ever built in the United States.

The Duesenberg engine was made by Lycoming and was remarkable in a day when most American cars had big L-headed lumps of cast iron under their hoods. The Duesenberg engine, in contrast, was based on the sort of power plants Fred Duesenberg had used in his racing machines. Its eight cylinders had a bore and stroke of 95 x 121 mm. Cubic capacity was

*Top left: Tom Alley driving a Duesenberg in
the 1914 Elgin, Illinois, races. Bottom left: Duesenberg
in which Jimmy Murphy won the French Grand
Prix in 1921. Famed driver Bob Burman
is at the wheel. Right: Supremely elegant town-car
body by Rollston on a Duesenberg SJ chassis.*

6,882 cc. Twin chain-driven overhead camshafts operated the inclined valves—four per cylinder—in fully machined hemispherical combustion chambers. Compression was typical for 1928—only 5.2 to 1. Higher-compression domed pistons were optional. The cylinder head was detachable. Pistons and connecting rods were of light alloy. The huge crankshaft was a masterly creation of heat-treated chrome-nickel steel and was statically and dynamically balanced. It weighed 150 pounds. To damp out torsional vibration two copper-lined cartridges 94 percent filled with mercury were bolted to opposite sides of the shaft between No. 1 and No. 2 cylinders. The shaft ran on only five main bearings and each was a hefty 2¾ inches in diameter. Good normal practice for a straight-eight engine would have required nine main bearings, but I have never heard of crankshaft failure due to a paucity of bearings in a Duesenberg engine, despite

Above: Three views of a 1933 Schwartz-bodied
SJ Duesenberg. The car cost only $17,500 in those days.
Note the elegant and well-filled instrument panel.
Opposite: Some still think that the Indianapolis-built
Duesenberg was a German car. This poster is from
a German importer of the American Duesenberg.

its 4,250 peak rpm—high for 1928.

Coil ignition from a 6-volt battery was standard. Early engines breathed through a twin-choke Schebler carburetor, but a down-draft manifold, usually with a Stromberg carburetor, was optional. Later on the down-draft carburetor was standardized.

The clutch, a specially designed double dry-plate type, transmitted power to a three-speed nonsynchromesh gearbox. Shifting was a somewhat clumsy chore. Downshifting for cornering or passing was not particularly satisfying. You just didn't play tunes on a Duesenberg transmission in order to enjoy yourself, as you might with a contemporary Bugatti or Alfa. A torque-tube drive and a silent hypoid spiral bevel rear end completed the drive line.

The chassis frame, mounted on leaf springs, was only slightly less robust than that under a Pullman car. The steel-alloy side members were no less than 8¼ inches deep and the steel was almost a quarter-inch thick. Six tubular cross members made for unusual rigidity. Despite a lot of aluminum in a Duesenberg chassis—crank chamber, dashboard, differential casing, camshaft covers—the weight of the super-strong frame and other robust components made a Duesenberg very heavy, indeed. An open touring car seldom weighed less than 5,000 pounds. A big limousine on the 153½-inch wheelbase of the long chassis frame might approach 7,000 pounds. The "short" chassis wheelbase was 142½ inches.

It wasn't easy to stop this great mass of moving metal, even with the big-drummed hydraulic brakes. Later models had a brake-booster that reduced the leg power needed.

The part of the Duesenberg that its driver saw most, its instrument panel, must surely have convinced him that he had got his money's worth. In addition to its usual instruments, it displayed not only an altimeter-barometer, a tachometer, a stopwatch-chronometer, and a brake-pressure gauge, but also an array of lights wired to a mysterious "black box." One light glowed every 750 miles to remind the operator to change the oil, another gleamed at 1,500-mile intervals to warn him that the storage

battery required topping up with water. Two other lights were wired to an engine-driven Bijur lubricator. If this was delivering oil to various distant outposts like the spring shackles, or hidden places like the clutch throwout bearing, a red light assured you that the oil was making its journey down the piping. If the oil reservoir was empty, a green light pricked your conscience.

How did a J Duesenberg perform? The company claimed that the engine developed 265 hp, that it had a top speed of 116 mph, and that it was capable of 90 mph in *second* gear. This would be a remarkable performance for a passenger car of fifty years ago. Perhaps the factory succeeded in reaching such speeds with a perfectly tuned, stripped-down, windshieldless example. Several times during the past thirty-odd years I have driven and been driven in various J's. They were fast, but by no means *that* fast. I've never seen 100 mph on the clock in any of them, and some of their conductors were really trying.

The supercharged versions of the Duesenberg, the SJ and the SSJ (the SSJ had a short wheelbase—125 inches), were said to be capable of 129 mph in high and 104 mph in second gear. Zero to 100 mph was said to take only seventeen seconds. The Duesenberg blower was a centrifugal type that rotated at astronomical speed—20,000 rpm when the engine was turning at 4,000 rpm. Five pounds per square inch at this speed was the purported boost.

At low engine revs the blower was quite ineffective. Blown engines were beefed up a bit with bigger crankshaft bearings, steel connecting rods, and stronger valve springs to withstand the stresses caused by the higher power developed. The supercharged SJ was credited by the company with no less than 320 bhp at 4,750 rpm.

The blown Duesenberg was identifiable by its external exhaust pipes. But J owners who desired the cachet of owning a supercharged car could have them installed on their blowerless machines.

August Duesenberg succeeded to the job of Chief Engineer after Fred was killed in a road accident in an SJ in 1932. In 1935 Augie decided to go in for some record-breaking. Famous long-distance driver Ab Jenkins took a special, light two-passenger SJ to the Bonneville Salt Flats. He had race driver Tony Gulotta along as his partner. On a 10-mile circular course the SJ took the international Class B hour record at 152.145 mph and the twenty-four-hour record at 135.47 mph. In 1936 the SJ engine was pulled out and a Curtiss Conquerer installed. A tailfin was added, too. The car was then named the Mormon Meteor I and took a fistful of records. Later, as the Mormon Meteor II, it broke further records. In 1938 the car became an almost-standard Duesenberg again after its SJ engine was put back in and fenders, door, and windshield were added. Jenkins then drove it for years afterward as a road car.

Like Rolls-Royce, Hispano-Suiza, and other such supercar makers, Duesenberg

Top: This 1925 straight-eight Model A Duesenberg roadster was better-looking than earlier Model A's. Bottom: SJ Duesenbergs with supercharged engines are recognizable by their external exhaust pipes. Such pipes were sometimes bought from the factory and fitted to unblown models by status-conscious owners.

did not build its own bodies. But if a customer wanted, say, a Rolls-Royce he could go to a dealer or body builder and have any kind of monstrosity built on a Rolls chassis, which Rolls would supply. Duesenberg wanted no such peculiar carriagework mounted on their chassis, and it was very difficult to buy one. In fact, almost no bare Duesenberg chassis were sold in this country. A few went to Europe, where bodies by Franay, Saoutchik, Fernandez and Darrin, Letournier et Marchand, and other famous *carrossiers* were built for them. In the United States, however, you usually placed your order for the kind of body you wanted directly with Duesenberg's design department, which created your body or let you choose one from a catalog that contained designs by such great American body builders as Murphy, Bohman and Schwartz, Locke, Derham, Le Baron, Dietrich, Rollston, and Brunn. One firm, La Grande, was controlled by Duesenberg. Duesenberg's chief designer for some years was the noted Gordon Buehrig, who was later responsible for the revolutionary 810 Cord. Bodies for Duesenbergs were not cheap by 1930's standards. A Murphy convertible roadster body cost almost $5,000. A limousine body was $7,500 or more. The "throne car" built for religious leader Father Divine cost far more. Chassis and body complete reputedly topped $25,000.

Who bought Duesenbergs? The very rich, of course, and the big-time movie types: Clark Gable, who bought them in quantity; Gary Cooper; Greta Garbo; Marion Davies and her friend William Randolph Hearst. Jimmy Walker owned one, as did marrying Tommy Manville. And I remember Bill "Bojangles" Robinson doing dance steps on and off the running board of his sedan when it was in Zumbach's for repair.

What was it like to drive a Duesenberg? I suppose that if you were used to driving big American arks in the 1930's—giant Packards, sixteen-cylinder Cadillacs, even Springfield Rolls-Royces—the Duesenberg was most impressive. It handled as well or better, and had rather more verve. Further, the Duesenberg was a joy to contemplate. No Duesenberg I've ever seen was ugly, and the view under a Duesenberg's hood was quite as pleasing as those under the hoods of Alfa Romeos or Bugattis.

But if Alfa Romeos or Bugattis were, in the 1930's, your kinds of car, you disdained Duesenbergs. For compared with a nervous and nimble Bug or Alfa, a Duesenberg was no more than a pretentious mobile monument. It was about as quick around a corner as one of the vast, fake, half-timbered Tudor mansions that so many Duesenberg owners inhabited. And if gear-shifting in a sports car was meant to be enjoyed, it was to be dreaded in a Duesenberg. That's why we didn't buy them in the late 1930's and 1940's, when they could be bought so very cheaply.

Am I sorry that I didn't buy that near-new convertible J in 1942 for $400? You bet I am. Even if I never drove it, I'd love to own a car now worth $150,000 or more.

*Top: This 1931 Model J Duesenberg Speedster
has unusual French headlights. Bottom: The Duesenberg
factory was determined to prevent any lesser
cars from colliding with one of its machines. The huge
stoplight not only glowed red but also
screamed "STOP" at tailgaters.*

Bugatti

The Bugatti was an individual and personal work of art conceived and executed by a master—Ettore Bugatti. The unique racing, sporting, and touring machines he designed and constructed not only handled and performed like no other motorcars, but every component of their finely sculpted mechanisms gave great joy to those who were sophisticated enough to appreciate them.

Ettore Bugatti was a north Italian, a Milanese, born in 1881. Carlo, his father, was a sculptor, architect, painter, and silversmith who was best known as a designer of highly original furniture. Ettore's brother Rembrandt was a sculptor, and Ettore himself was sent off to study at the Brera Art Academy. But something besides art had captured his seventeen-year-old imagination—those stuttering, clattering, motorized devices that could occasionally be seen moving through the streets of Milan.

We don't know what painful arguments took place in the Bugatti household, but Ettore soon became an apprentice in the shops of Prunetti and Stucchi, where within a year he produced a twin-engined tricycle. Of course, the eighteen-year-old immediately had to go racing on his pride and joy. He won eight out of the ten local events he entered.

Those were the days of the great town-to-town and country-to-country road races. In May, 1899, Bugatti had the gall to enter his tricycle in the Paris-Bordeaux race in which the great cracks of Europe—De Knyff, Jarrot, Charron, Girardot—were running their Panhards, De Dietrichs, and Mors. Bugatti's tricycle competed in the motorcycle class against thirty-six other two- and three-wheelers. At Poitiers, the end of the first stage, he was lying third, having passed thirty-three motorcyclists. But he failed to run in the next stage, having badly bent his machine in an affray with a dog.

Bugatti seems at that time to have been hooked on multiengined vehicles. The small device he next built had no fewer than four small engines. As might be expected, he had gear-shifting difficulties and designed still another car. This one was never built. For Prunetti and Stucchi quit the car business in favor of manufacturing sewing machines.

With the superconfidence of youth and without any technical training beyond his short apprenticeship—and certainly without the label of *Ingegnere*—Bugatti decided that he would manufacture cars on his own. His father, not realizing that he had a mechanical genius on his hands, turned him down when he asked for financial backing.

Still, a pair of perceptive counts, the Gulinelli brothers, recognized young Bugatti's abilities when he enthusiastically showed them his designs for an advanced new car. He showed them drawings, explained how the machine would be built, and convinced them that in spite of his youth he knew whereof he spoke. They put up the money. And if the nobility thought

Preceding pages: The 1932 Type 55 Bugatti was a tough supersports version of the Type 51 Grand Prix machine and was powered by a supercharged 2.3-liter engine. The car's suspension was quite as spine-jarring as that of the Grand Prix car. The lovely body was designed by Jean Bugatti.

so much of his son, how could Papa Carlo hang back? He put up some lire, too.

Ettore not only turned out the working drawings, he also carved the wooden patterns for the castings and helped the mechanics with the hand-fitting. The car ran beautifully at the then high speed of 40 mph. At the ripe old age of nineteen, Bugatti was at last an *Ingegnere* and the top man at the Bugatti-Gulinelli Motor Company. This first Bugatti-designed car was shown at the International Exhibition in Milan in 1901. It got a medal from the Automobile Club of France and the City Cup. Ettore was invited to Niedebronn in Alsace for an interview with Baron Eugène de Dietrich, head of the company that built the excellent De Dietrich automobiles. The upshot was the offer of a contract. Ettore was to license De Dietrich to build his cars. But he was still a minor, and Papa had to countersign the agreement.

Bugatti had to move to Alsace in order to work at the De Dietrich factory and for most of the next forty-five years he lived and worked in that oddly Franco-German part of Europe.

Ettore Bugatti didn't produce cars bearing his own name until 1910. Until then he designed automobiles for Hermes, Deutz, Mathis, Peugeot, and perhaps Isotta Fraschini.

It was in the town of Molsheim that Bugatti set up his home and his factory. In the years to come that obscure little place near Strasbourg would become famous for the remarkable motorcars that were born there.

The years between the wars were the great times of the super-Bugattis. But even before World War I, when Alsace was still a German province, there were already Bugattis whose unique characteristics foretold the future of the marque. The first of these was the Type 13 of 1910 (which with variations in dimensions and other details was also known as Types 15, 17, 22, and 23).

In a day when expensive cars were imposingly large and fitted with big-bellied engines, it surprised people to be confronted with a quite expensive but tiny machine like the Type 13. Very small cars were expected to be very cheap, and that first Bugatti had only a 79-inch wheelbase, a 45-inch track, and weighed but 750 pounds, which almost doubled when its two occupants and its fuel and water were aboard. Its four-cylinder 1,327-cc engine had eight valves driven by an overhead camshaft (as in every Bugatti ever built). Only 25 bhp were developed, but the car was capable of 60 mph.

"Jewellike" is a term I have perhaps overused when writing about the precise construction and finish of Bugattis. Yet the Type 13 of 1910 was already worthy of that description. Engine, four-speed gearbox, multiplate clutch, and rear axle were pure Bugatti.

It didn't take long for Bugatti to engage his car in racing. And racing in those days meant taking on the big-engined behemoths that dominated Europe's road circuits. In a race at Le Mans in July, 1911, a tiny 750-pound Type 13 driven by Bugatti's friend Ernest Friderich

came in second to a big brute of a Fiat driven by the great Victor Hemery. Behind the elegant little Bugatti was a gaggle of big cars, including one driven by Gabriel, the famous driver of the Mors in the 1903 Paris-Madrid.

The race spurred the growing awareness that Bugatti was building cars to hitherto unknown standards of perfection and if business didn't exactly boom, sophisticated buyers nonetheless began buying his cars in satisfying numbers. He began building various new models, among them a machine unusually large for Bugatti. This had a four-cylinder, 5-liter overhead-camshaft engine and, remarkably, chain drive. A version with shaft drive ran at the Indianapolis 500 in 1914. Although it was in second place for a time, it fell out with bearing failure.

Alsace was German in 1914. Bugatti was an Italian but his sympathies were French. Before the armies started marching, Bugatti, his wife, his three children, and two racing cars made it to Stuttgart and then to Friedrichshafen. With the help of his friend Count Zeppelin, the airship builder, Bugatti and his family at last made it to Milan. The two racing Bugattis were stashed in a wet cellar, which did them no good. Three other cars had been buried at Molsheim, where the Germans never found them. They were resurrected four years later.

Bugatti offered his invention of a quick-firing cannon to his countrymen, but they turned him down. He did, however, get permission to go to Paris to try interesting the French in his gun. They couldn't have cared

Preceding pages: Front and rear views of the 1932 Type 55 Bugatti. Above: 1927 Type 43 Grand Sport Bugatti had a 2.3-liter, 100-hp, supercharged engine that was a slightly detuned version of that in the Type 35B Grand Prix car. The Type 43 was remarkably quick for its day—over 110 mph.

less. In Paris Bugatti was able to round up those of his draftsmen and mechanics who had been able to make it from Molsheim. He set up a workshop and was soon designing airplane engines. The rights to a double-eight, 500-hp engine were bought by the United States and it was put into production at the Duesenberg factory in Elizabeth, New Jersey.

It was in the 1920's that the Bugatti became one of the world's supercars. When Ettore returned to Molsheim he dug up the cars he had buried in 1914 and he had the two water-damaged machines brought back from Milan. Rebuilt and refurbished, these old Type 13 machines soon started to win races. At Brescia modified versions with ball-bearing crankshafts, sixteen valves, capacity increased to 1,496 cc, and slightly longer wheelbases came in first, second, third, and fourth. That's how that model became known as the Brescia. It was an immediate success. British and Continental competition drivers fell all over themselves to get hold of those that Bugatti released for private sale. One British driver, the famous Raymond Mays, as yet not too well known in 1923, bought one and campaigned it in various hill climbs. But he and his friend Amherst Villiers, who later designed the supercharger for the "blower" Bentley, felt that the Bugatti could do with higher revs and more power. They had the temerity to modify the Bugatti engine and were soon winning every British hill climb in sight.

Ettore, hearing about Mays's successes, invited him and Villiers to Molsheim. There he asked Mays to carry out some acceleration and speed tests on the main Molsheim-Strasbourg road.

In his excellent book *Split Seconds*, Mays describes what happened: "The little Bugatti was on top of its form and never before had Ettore Bugatti heard so many revs and such an exhaust note from one of his cars. He seemed very thrilled and expressed a wish to drive the car back to the works with me as passenger. Little did I know what I had let myself in for. It was the most hectic and terrifying ride I have ever had—Bugatti seemed to drive flat out everywhere, corners and straights alike. In a flash something crossed the road in front of us; to avoid this Bugatti drove off the road, quite unperturbed, on to the grass and round the back of a tree—still with his foot hard down. Soon, thank heaven, the engine suddenly stopped—never in my life was I so pleased to find that we had run out of fuel! Bugatti was delighted with the car and agreed to allow Amherst Villiers to remain at the works for several weeks to assist in rebuilding the old car and preparing the new one. The following morning I set off for England by train."

Ettore grandly presented Mays with a new car for his trouble. Mays named his two Brescias Cordon Rouge and Cordon Bleu, and for the next few years they were almost unbeatable in hill climbs.

A delectable sports version of the Brescia, the Brescia Modifié, appeared in 1924. With four-wheel brakes, a starter, and lights, it

Top: 4.9-liter, supercharged, twin-overhead-camshaft straight-eight engine of the Type 50T Bugatti developed 150 hp. Note the typical Bugatti square-cut and fettled cam box. Bottom: The 2.3-liter blown engine of the Type 55 had half the capacity of that in the 50T but developed only slightly less power—135 hp.

made most other sporting vehicles of its time seem old-fashioned. Present-day owners of Brescias still derive great joy from them.

By the 1920's the Brescia was a car from a different age, the world of pre-1914. Still, it was the precursor of a different kind of motorcar, the lighter, more precisely built, higher-revving machines of the hectic time between the two world wars. And Ettore Bugatti, during those twenty years, built automobiles that no one has yet surpassed in originality and beauty of construction.

Bugatti created his masterpieces in as remarkable a milieu as ever saw the construction of motorcars. His factory, his house, his hobbies, his work people, his horses, his dogs, were all part of a fiefdom, and Ettore was its reigning prince. Behind great varnished oak doors, each with its bronze lock, were a winery, a distillery for kirsch, a museum for his brother Rembrandt's sculptures. There were stables for Ettore's thoroughbreds, a boat-building yard, a riding academy, an aviary, a carriage museum. And for customers come to take delivery of their cars (for which they had to pay spot cash), there was a hotel, the Hostellerie du Pur Sang. One tile-lined building was a generating station—Bugatti had decided to make his own electricity after he got fed up with the power company (as who of us hasn't).

But the living center of all this was the *usine*—the factory. Spotless, with wood-block floors, it was in sharp contrast to the almost medieval look of the rest of Bugatti's do-

Top: A 1 1/2-liter Brescia Bugatti of about 1923. Note the front-wheel brakes. Bottom: A Type 41 "Royale" Bugatti. This car had no headlights because the owner said he didn't intend to drive at night.

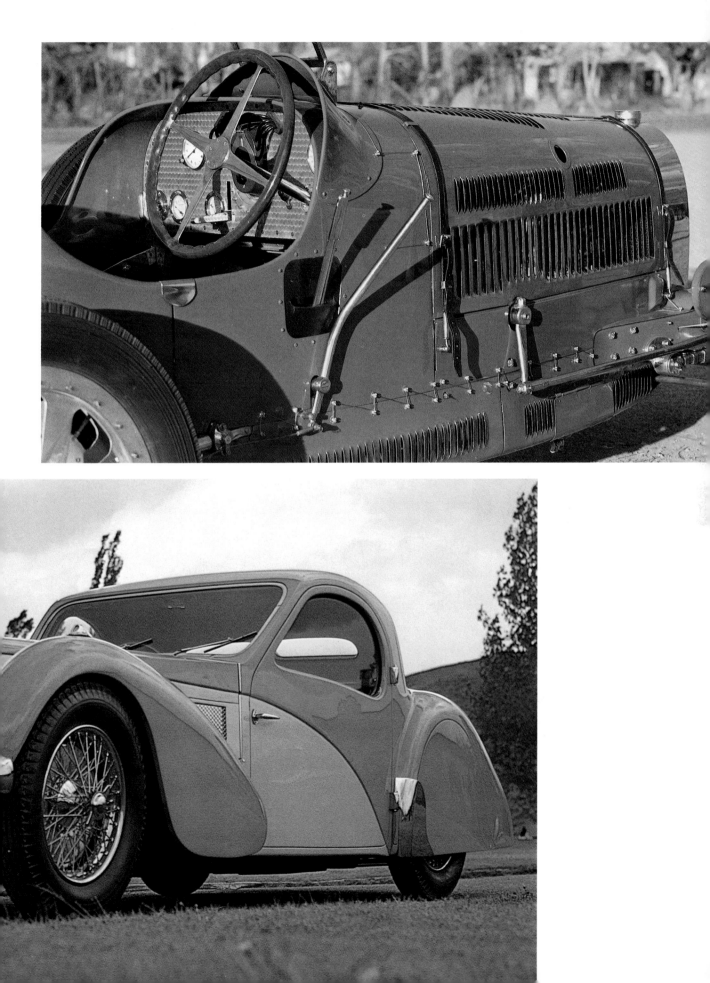

main. In splendid array was automatic machinery of the latest types then available—Swiss lathes, American machine tools, special machines devised by Ettore, dynamometers. And on the fitters' benches, vises proudly emblazoned "Bugatti." Pity the poor fellow who marred one with a file.

Le Patron, as Bugatti liked to be addressed, surveyed his little principality from the saddle of a bicycle, one of many he, of course, designed himself. Disdaining those he could buy, he continually thought up new kinds of lightweight velocipedes in steel or aluminum. This writer never saw him aboard a bicycle but did once see him conducting an electric-powered, tiller-steered device like a bath chair. At the time he was wearing a light tan pongee suit, a yellow waistcoat, and a brown bowler. He was being conservative that day.

Bugatti's first really new postwar passenger car was the Type 30 of 1923. It had a 1,990-cc straight-eight engine, the type of power plant most notably associated with the Bugatti marque.

The engine in the Type 30 was the first to have that austere, sharp-edged, slablike look that would later be common to all single-ohc Bugattis. It had three valves per cylinder, a ball-bearing crankshaft (but with babbitted rod bearings), and twin Zenith carburetors (later cars had only one carburetor). An oddity of the chassis was its peculiar four-wheel braking system—hydraulic in the front and mechanical aft. The touring Type 30 was not the greatest of

Bugattis. Very similar racing machines built in 1922 before the touring model appeared had competed with rather mixed results.

Four such Bugattis were entered in the 1922 French Grand Prix at Strasbourg. They were the second ugliest Le Patron ever let out of Molsheim (the ugliest were the tank-bodied jobs—the Type 32's, which ran in the same race a year later). They had peculiar round noses, which looked as if they were surplus fighter-airplane cowls bought cheap, and revolting-looking skinny tails. The exhaust escaped through a hole in the end of the tail. Yet of the eighteen cars that started—Fiats, Sunbeams, Ballots, and so on—only four finished the race, three of them Bugattis right behind Felice Nazzaro, the winner on a Fiat.

In 1923 five of the Bugattis were entered in the Indianapolis 500. One, driven by a Prince de Cystria, finished ninth. Most of the failed Bugattis went out because of bearing failure caused by Bugatti's use of an archaic lubrication system that squirted oil on the bearings. Ettore persisted in using this system until 1929, when he at last adopted pressure lubrication.

Later in 1923 Bugatti ran those aforementioned aerodynamic "tanks" in the French Grand Prix. These Type 32's had straight-eight engines much like those in the Type 30, but with roller-bearing crankshafts. Three of the little 79-inch-wheelbase Bugattis started. One, driven by Ettore's old friend Friderich, came in third. Bugatti didn't permanently abandon tanklike bodywork. His simi-

Preceding pages, top left: The 1932 Type 50T Bugatti's blown 4.9-liter engine gave it a top speed of over 100 mph. Top right: "Office" of the Type 35B Grand Prix Bugatti. Bottom left: White elephant radiator ornament of the Type 41 Royale model. Bottom right: 1937 Type 57SC Atalante coupe was the ultimate development of the Type 57.

larly shaped cars won at Le Mans in 1937 and again in 1939. Later, his famous high-speed railcars had similarly shaped head ends.

Ettore had something else on his drawing board, the most successful racing car of his career. And it *was* Ettore's drawing board, for he did not depend on others to create his cars. Sketching in the round, in three dimensions, Bugatti designed all of his cars right down to their smallest components. And he worked rapidly. It took him only a day or two to work out extremely complex mechanisms. When flat working drawings for the toolmakers or machinists were required he employed draftsmen, but he insisted that they too should be able to draw in perspective, like artists.

At times there were problems with the drawings Le Patron dashed off. Some of the parts he drew were not robust enough. At fault were the eyeglasses he wore when drawing. These spectacles (which he, of course, had designed himself) magnified what he was looking at. The things he sketched looked bigger to him than they actually were!

It was the great Type 35 Grand Prix Bugatti that came from Ettore's pencil in 1924. It was built to be raced not only by the factory, but by anyone who came to Molsheim with enough francs in his hot little hand (100,000—about $6,000). And the cars Monsieur Bugatti sold were much the same as those that the factory campaigned.

The first Type 35 had a straight-eight engine not unlike that in the G. P. version of the Type 30—1,900 cc. The nickel-chrome steel crankshaft was now built up in sections to accommodate ball bearings for the mains, and roller bearings for the connecting rods. The two inlet valves and the single exhaust valve for each cylinder were operated by a single overhead camshaft driven by a vertical shaft at the front of the engine. The head was, of course, not detachable. Twin Zenith carburetors provided sustenance for the Type 35. Lubrication was still provided by those jets that spat oil on the moving parts. An unblown Type 35 engine developed some 90 bhp, and 110 mph was easily attainable.

Assume that you are viewing a Type 35. If you can tear yourself away from admiring the lovely-looking Bugatti engine, stand back and look at the car as a whole. Aesthetically, it would seem impossible to change a line of it. The distribution of its chief masses, the wedge-shaped tail, the subtle curve of the top of the hood, the size of the wheels in relation to the rest of the machine, are all just right. The details—the horseshoe-shaped radiator (from Ettore's equine enthusiasm); the splendidly sculptured hollow, solid-ended, polished steel front axle through whose square apertures the front springs pass; the polished, flat-spoked, aluminum wheels—all are sheer delight. Even the red, white, and black oval Bugatti badge is just right.

The front ends of the chassis members seem impossibly fragile. They are a mere three-quarters of an inch deep. But the chassis, which follows the boat-shaped curve of the

body, is strong enough where it counts. Under the dash it is 6 inches deep. The chassis is suspended on half-elliptic springs in front and almost immovable quarter-elliptics aft.

The cast-aluminum wheels are not made that way for looks. The brake drums are cast into them. During a race, changing a wheel makes it possible to renew the drum, too. Further, the brake shoes become instantly visible and changeable.

Five Type 35's were entered in the European Grand Prix run at Lyons in August, 1924. Against them was a formidable array of Delages, Sunbeams, Alfa Romeos, Fiats, and a Miller. Ettore showed up at the race in his usual expansive style. The cars were driven to Lyons. A special train carried spare parts, food, wine, a huge tent for the mechanics, and a house trailer for the Bugatti *ménage*.

But Le Patron made a mistake. He had ordered specially designed tires that he thought would be more secure on the aluminum wheels (which in those days had detachable rims). Almost immediately after the start the tires, too new to be sufficiently cured, started to disintegrate. The best the Bugattis could do was seventh and eighth place.

But it wasn't long before the luck of the Bugattis changed. Soon the cars were winning race after race. In various forms they won more races than any racing cars of all time. During the next few years they won almost a thousand times. They were not always important races, but enough of them were Grands Prix.

The 2-liter Type 35 of 1924 was the progenitor of other Type 35's and also of various sports cars based on the same chassis. The Type 35A of 1925, the *"course imitation,"* was a cheaper version of the Grand Prix machine. Its crankshaft still revolved on ball bearings but its connecting-rod bearings were babbitted instead of being roller bearings. Instead of a magneto, a Delco coil and distributor were fitted. And since it was anticipated that users might drive it as a road car, the instrument panel carried a headlight switch. Wire wheels replaced the cast-aluminum type, and it was therefore necessary to install normal brake drums. British friends have on occasion referred to this simplified Type 35 as a "boys' racer," but it was only slightly less potent than the Grand Prix version. It was easily capable of 100 mph.

The Type 35C of 1927 was a supercharged version of the 2-liter Type 35. Its Roots blower boosted its horsepower to 130. It was capable of 125 mph. The Type 35T of 1927 was a Grand Prix machine with a longer stroke than the original Type 35. It had a 2.3-liter (60 x 100-mm) engine and put out 130 bhp. It was unblown. The Type 35B was the *ne plus ultra* of the Type 35's. With a supercharger and 2.3 liters, it was the most puissant of the 35's—140 bhp and 130 mph.

There were several close relatives of the Type 35's that, externally, were almost indistinguishable from their sisters. The Type 37 of 1925 was a 1,500-cc four-cylinder version that in blown form was called the Type 37A. Both

Lushly swooping fenders were typical of the cars designed by Ettore Bugatti's son Jean. Here they appear on a pair of 1932 Bugatti sports cars. The upper one is a big Type 50T. Below it is the Type 55 two-seater. It's hard to believe that they were designed almost a half-century ago.

usually had wire wheels. The 37 could exceed 95 mph; the 37A could get up to 110 or so.

The Type 39 of 1926 and the 39A of 1927 were straight eights with only 1,500-cc capacity. Both were Grand Prix machines. The 39A was supercharged. The Type 39 developed 80 bhp and was capable of no less than 105 mph. The 39A with 120 bhp was some 20 mph quicker.

In 1929 Le Patron decided that the heads of his cars ought to be embellished with two camshafts instead of one. An American race driver, Leon Duray, had brought a pair of Indianapolis-type race cars to Europe. These had twin-cam Miller engines that Bugatti wanted to study. A swap was arranged, and Ettore got the Miller-engined cars in trade for three Type 43 sports cars.

Soon there appeared the supercharged Type 51 Grand Prix car with twin camshafts à la Miller. The 51, which was almost identical to a Type 35B, except for its engine, was capable of 140 mph from 180 bhp.

I've had a bit of experience with a Type 51. In 1936 one was entered in the revived Vanderbilt Cup Race at Roosevelt Field on Long Island. The American driver chosen to conduct the Bugatti was terrified of its gearbox. Fearing to shift out of second speed, he over-revved, thus poking a connecting rod through the side of its crankcase. A friend, Leo Pavelle, and I bought the ailing Bugatti for $400. We took it to Zumbach's, the foreign-car repairers in New York, for treatment. When the engine

was dismembered it became clear that the con rod was not the first to have escaped its confines. The previous owner(s) had had similar problems. Further, in addition to the rod and its roller bearing, the crankshaft journal was also in a parlous state. Zumbach's disassembled the shaft and sent the affected parts to Molsheim. After a few months, a neatly made wooden box containing the parts arrived and Zumbach's put things back together.

The car ran beautifully. But since it had no lights, top fenders, or starter, we had to avoid using the beast at night or in the rain. I remember stalling it once or twice in New York traffic, to the glee of taxi drivers.

We should, I think, have sent the whole engine to the factory so that Bugatti's experts could have reassembled it. In any case, Leo, revving in second gear one day to defeat a Chevrolet that was challenging the Bugatti at a tollbooth, put the same rod through the side of the crankcase again. We sold the Bugatti to a wretch who replaced its lovely engine with, of all horrid things, a Peerless marine engine.

Many owners in the 1930's ran their Type 35's as sports cars, complete with lights and fenders. It was even possible in those days to buy a cradlelike device that held an electric starter.

But there was a better way. In 1927 Bugatti produced one of the most desirable supersports cars of all time: the Type 43 Grand Sport based on the Type 35B 2.3-liter supercharged racing machine. The Type 43's engine was the same blown straight eight with a slightly lower compression ratio. It developed 115 bhp. It was mounted in a chassis long enough to accommodate as lovely a four-passenger boat-tailed body as ever made a car enthusiast's heart beat faster.

For its time, the Type 43 had an almost miraculous performance: over 110 mph and zero to 60 mph in under twelve seconds. Only a Grand Prix machine could equal it in roadholding or steering. I can think of no car of its time whose constructional details could give its driver such joy—for the 1,750-cc blown Gran Sport Alfa Romeo was still in the future.

The three cars that Leon Duray got in the trade he made for his Miller-engined cars were all Type 43's—one with the open boat-tailed body, two with rather heavy-looking though beautiful convertible bodies. In the early thirties they were displayed in a New York shop window. The asking price was $1,500 each. I've never wanted a car more than that Grand Sport Type 43, but I hadn't the wherewithal. The usual price for a Type 43 was about $7,500 in New York. A slightly less potent version of the Type 43 was produced in 1930—the Type 43A roadster with 100 bhp and a 100-mph speed.

The other great Bugatti supersports machine was the Type 55, which like the 43 was also based on a Grand Prix machine—the twin-overhead-camshaft Type 51. The Type 55, which appeared in 1932, had a straight-eight, 2.3-liter supercharged engine that put out 135 bhp at 5,500 rpm. The chassis was the same as that of the Grand Prix Type 49. The delightful swoop-fendered roadster body was designed by Ettore's son Jean and was unusual for a sports car of the time in allowing the driver (and his passenger) to sit up as if he were in a comfortable chair instead of lying supine with his legs stretched out. This was accomplished by putting the pedals in surprisingly deep footwells.

For 1932 the performance of a Type 55 was downright shattering: zero to 60 mph in under ten seconds, a top speed near 120 mph, and 100 mph in the third gear of its tough, four-speed gearbox. Such performance was almost unimaginable in the 1930's. The Type 55 was no quiet pussycat of a car. It made wonderful noises. Its Roots blower, its straight-toothed gears, its exhaust "like the tearing of calico," all added up to a most exhilarating cacophony. Its stiff suspension, unameliorated by the quarter-elliptic rear springs, added to the driver's feeling that he was conducting a near-racing *bolide*. And this flurry of noise and vibration and speed terrified any passenger unused to such a combination of excitements.

When an acquaintance took me out in his Type 55 one night in about 1933, I said something silly like, "As you know, I'm used to sports cars since I own a 22/90 Alfa Romeo." But that Type 55 was something else again. It made that old Alfa seem as gentle as a hearse. Especially when the driver treated all other cars on the two-lane roads like so many stationary objects through which he steered a slightly snaking course. The 55 had so much power, so much

*Cockpit of the 1932 Type 55 Bugatti roadster.
Occupants sat with their feet in deep footwells, making
it unnecessary to assume the supine position required
in most sports cars. Note that the macho owner
of this machine disdains the use of a full windshield
and depends on a minuscule aero screen.*

speed and acceleration compared with the V-8 Fords and Nashes and Franklins that he could ignore them with impunity. The road was his. Always.

Ettore Bugatti produced some seven thousand cars between 1910 and 1939. Of these only about five hundred were out-and-out racing and supersports machines. The rest were touring machines of varying degrees of potency.

The least sporting of Bugatti's cars was the Type 44, sometimes put down as *"La Buick de Molsheim."* But not everyone wanted the nervous, noisy, and sometimes fussy near-racing models. Of all the touring and sports Bugattis ever built more people bought the Type 44 than any other model—twelve hundred of them.

The Type 44, which appeared in 1927, had a straight-eight, 3-liter engine with the usual single overhead camshaft. A single Schebler carburetor was fitted. It put out about 80 bhp. Despite being a "cooking" version as compared with some other Bugatti engines, it was finished in the usual Bugatti style.

A man I used to meet at Zumbach's owned a fine example of the 44 with a four-passenger, English-built fabric body. And one day in the late 1930's he was nice enough to let me take a turn at the wheel of his pampered darling.

I drove it for half an hour or so in New York's Central Park. It was a lovely, quiet machine, but certainly no Buick. It steered impeccably, didn't roll Buick-wise on corners, and had a typically precise Bugatti four-speed gearbox. But somehow Ettore had contrived things so that the machine, unlike some of his sportier models, didn't require much gear-shifting. If you wished to drive it in un-Bugatti-ish fashion you could crawl along at ridiculously low speeds in top gear. Top speed was about 80 mph.

The Type 44 was a comparatively simple Bugatti. Its crankshaft ran on nine babbitted main bearings instead of the five ball bearings of, say, a Type 35B. It had no supercharger and it was not a recalcitrant starter on a cold morning.

Perhaps this is why some dedicated Bugattistes look down on the Type 44. They boast about the painstaking drill they go through before asking their cars' engines to commence on a cold morning. A religious Bugattiphile pretends that he loves to drain the oil and water from his engine and warm them on the kitchen range before dribbling these vital fluids through filters back into the engine. He removes and carefully checks each spark plug. Then he carefully turns the engine with the starting crank to distribute the oil before he subjects it to the brutality of the electric starter. And if on occasion he takes his engine apart, he's careful, if it's an early one and has that archaic Bugatti system of oil jets that spit lubricant at the revolving crankshaft, not to use the kind of rag that might impede one of the jets with a tiny bit of lint. (Early 44's had such oil jets. Later ones used a proper pressure system.)

The Type 44 was perhaps the machine for the moderately well-to-do bourgeois who hoped that people might think him a dash-

*3.3-liter Type 57C Bugatti Atalante coupe was a
supercharged version of the Type 57 Normale. Both had a higher
chassis than the ultralow supersports Type 57S and 57SC
models. A blown 160-hp Type 57C was capable of about 105 mph.
The author tried to dissuade the man at the wheel from
buying it in 1951, saying $1,500 was too high a price.*

ing fellow indeed as he paraded, complete with his white cloth helmet, along the *grands boulevards* in a car not too unlike the one that had just won the Grand Prix. If our man got richer he bought himself other, faster touring machines: the 5-liter Types 46 and 46S (supercharged) of 1930, the Type 49 of 1929, which was a slightly larger version of the Type 44, or even the superfast, superluxurious, twin-overhead-camshaft supercharged 5-liter Type 50T of 1932, which was capable of over 100 mph.

If, however, our man was a veritable Croesus, he might already have the most formidable, biggest, most expensive car in the world. This was the Royale, the Type 41, the Golden Bug. Ettore built this supercar to outluxury all the other supercars—the Rolls-Royce, the Hispano-Suiza, the Isotta Fraschini. (Pity he couldn't give his machine a double-barreled name, too.) Ettore, something of a snob, loved royalty and titles, and he constructed the Royale for the use and edificaton of kings, a few of whom still infested Europe in 1927. Sadly, no such crowned head ever bought one of the six Golden Bugs that were completed.

The Royale was of gargantuan proportions. Its wheelbase was 169 inches, its track 66 inches. It weighed over 7,000 pounds and it stood on wheels that used 7.50 x 24 tires. Its straight-eight, 13-liter engine (overhead cam, of course) developed almost 300 bhp at a mere 1,700 rpm. With that kind of power and torque Ettore might have saved himself the trouble of furnishing a gearbox at all. But he installed one

in the rear axle anyway. It had three speeds: low for moving away from rest if the driver was confronted with a clifflike grade, second speed for all normal starting and running, and an overdrive for really high speed, necessary perhaps if His Majesty in the back seat found it imperative to outdistance subjects bent on regicide. Over 125 mph was possible. A Royale chassis cost 500,000 francs, about $30,000 in 1927, equal to some $150,000 in today's currency.

A few years ago I was taken for a run in one of the two Royales owned by Harrah's Automobile Collection in Reno, Nevada. Despite having a *coupe de ville* body it had everything you'd expect in a Bugatti: polished, hollow front axle, quarter-elliptic springs aft, the hard Bugatti sound (although somewhat muffled), and the clean monolithic engine. Mr. Harrah's driver handled it like a Bugatti (except that he didn't play tunes on the gearbox), whipping it around corners as if it were a Type 35.

Car repairers in New York in the 1930's were not too crazy about working on Bugattis. Since Bugatti engines had nondetachable cylinder heads, which had the obvious virtue of eliminating gasket troubles, it was necessary to lift the engine block out of the car if the valves required attention. Some models—the Type 46, for example—had their gearboxes in their rear axles and it was necessary to detach the axle from the rear springs in order to do something as simple as grinding the valves. The Royale's crankshaft, which was over 4 feet long and weighed 220 pounds, had first to be removed before the huge cylinder block could be hoisted out. A valve job on a Royale cost rather more than the price of a new Ford. And labor costs were about a tenth of what they are now. In the thirties Zumbach's charged only $1.50 an hour for work on foreign cars.

During the early 1930's Bugatti's domination of Grand Prix racing rapidly waned. The Italian Alfa Romeos and Maseratis, with liberal infusions of money from Mussolini's fascist government, became almost unbeatable. During the late 1930's the Mercedes-Benz and Auto-Union teams, racing for the greater glory of Hitler's Third Reich and therefore liberally supplied with marks, made it almost impossible for either Bugatti or Alfa Romeo to win races.

Bugatti, without government backing, still persevered. The 4.9-liter Type 54 was the first new Grand Prix machine to be pitted against the Italians. It was a heavy, unwieldy machine, dangerous to drive, and had only limited success.

The last Grand Prix car built by Bugatti was the classically elegant Type 59. Unlike the rather characterless-looking German and Italian machines that were shaped very differently from their ancestors, the Type 59 was indubitably a Bugatti from its horseshoe radiator to its quarter-elliptic rear springs.

The Type 59 had a twin-overhead-camshaft, straight-eight engine much like that in the Type 57 touring car. Both the touring Type 57 and the racing 59 came out in 1934. At first the Type 59 had a 2.8-liter engine, but its capacity was soon increased to 3.3 liters. Compared with the German and Italian Grand Prix cars, the Type 59's chassis was downright old-fashioned, for Ettore had eschewed independent suspension in favor of splitting the typical Bugatti front axle and joining the halves with a collar. He maintained that this gave each front wheel a modicum of independence, but it really did nothing at all. He did use a dreadfully complex and very expensive type of shock absorber to help keep the Type 59's unusual piano-wire wheels in better contact with the road. These De Ram shock absorbers hydraulically tightened themselves in relation to the car's speed.

I once saw a couple of these Type 59's in action at a rather minor race, the Grand Prix de Deauville in 1936. There wasn't much opposition, and a 59 driven by Jean Pierre Wimille won. During a pit stop one of the Type 59's balked at starting. The lowliest mechanic in the pit crew wound the peculiar side-mounted starting handle to no avail. The next man tried. No luck. Then the *chef* gave it his all. The engine started, but the mechanic fell over in a dead faint, his white coveralls spotted with his blood. Two ambulance men hauled him away on a stretcher as Ettore Bugatti, who was standing near me, looked on without even a flicker of interest.

But Ettore, in 1936, had bigger troubles than slightly recalcitrant racing cars. Bugatti had always considered himself a sort of liege lord to his work people. He assumed that they had an uncritical love for him. He was

Beautiful from any aspect, the Type 35B Grand Prix model was the quintessential Bugatti. The famous hollow, polished front axle and the aluminum flat-spoked wheels are shown at their best here. Its 140-hp blown 2.3-liter engine gave it a speed of 130 mph.

amazed and hurt when, like millions of other workers in France in 1936, his loyal subjects declared a sit-down strike. Bugatti in his lordly fashion refused to negotiate with the strikers and departed from Molsheim. Even after the strike was over, the place had somehow lost its charm for him and he rarely returned. He handed over the management to his son Jean. Bugatti set up his office at his showroom on the Avenue Montaigne in Paris.

Jean Bugatti had much to do with the design and production of the several Type 57's that were the greatest of Bugatti's touring machines and which formed the basis for the cars that twice won the twenty-four-hour Le Mans race.

The first Type 57 appeared in 1934 to the accompaniment of a certain amount of growling by old-time Bugattistes (mostly British) that Bugatti had grown soft at last, that he had given up his tough, noisy, manly machines and was now turning out a quiet car for softies. This, of course, was quite untrue. The Type 57 was all *pur sang* Bugatti. True, it was more refined. But it was notably quick in its more sporting guises and gave away nothing to earlier Bugattis in nimble handling, roadholding, and excitement.

The Type 57 had a 3.3-liter twin-overhead-camshaft straight-eight engine built in the expected uncompromisingly perfect Bugatti style. The four-speed "crash-type" gearbox was built integrally with the engine, in contrast with other Bugatti transmissions that had either been separate from the engine and mounted amidships or in the rear axle. The chassis had the usual polished front axle, semielliptic springs forward and quarter-elliptics aft. At first, brakes were cable-operated. Later brakes were hydraulics. The Type 57 *normale* was capable of about 95 mph from its 130 bhp. The supercharged Type 57C, which came out in 1936, had 160 bhp and a top speed of 105 mph. The Type 57S of 1936 was unblown but was shorter and lower. Its engine had a lighter crankshaft and higher-compression pistons than the *normales* and it put out about 190 bhp. The complex and expensive De Ram shock absorbers were fitted to this brilliant model, capable of over 125 mph.

The ultimate Type 57 was the 57SC, which had the low chassis of the 57S *and* a Roots supercharger. It could exceed 135 mph from its 220 bhp. Only a few were built.

In 1937 a 57S and in 1939 a 57C, clothed in massive bodies reminiscent of the "tanks" of 1923, won at Le Mans.

In August, 1939, Jean Bugatti took a 57C tank-bodied car out to test it on a road near Molsheim. As usual, men were placed at each end of the road to warn off traffic. But a drunken postman on a bicycle wobbled onto the highway. At high speed, young Bugatti swerved to avoid hitting the drunk, but he crashed and was killed. He was thirty years old. Within a few days Ettore, still stunned with grief, again had to try to evacuate the factory as the Germans massed to invade France.

When the war started Bugatti

This 1951 Type 101 Bugatti was built at Molsheim after Ettore Bugatti's death. It was basically a Type 57 with a 3.3-liter engine and could be supplied either with or without a supercharger. It had Weber carburetors and chain-driven camshafts. Very few 101's were built.

stealthily transported his machinery to Bordeaux to manufacture parts for Hispano-Suiza airplane engines. But by June, 1940, France was finished and the Germans insisted that Bugatti work for them. In November, 1940, the Bordeaux factory was bombed by the RAF, and the Germans, accusing Bugatti of conniving with the British, barred him from the factory. Bugatti went to Paris, where during the war years he turned out designs for new cars, boats, and marine engines.

When the war ended, Bugatti, who had never given up his Italian citizenship, was accused of collaborating with the Nazis. The French government seized what was left of the war-damaged Molsheim factory as enemy property. Bugatti appealed and the courts upheld him. But at sixty-six Bugatti was tired out. His wife had died during the war. He died in August, 1947.

In 1951 a new Bugatti was exhibited at the Paris show. This Type 101 was built at Molsheim, which was then managed by Pierre Marco, a long-time associate of Bugatti. The Type 101 engine was much like that of the Type 57. The bodies were beautifully built but unfortunately in the idiom of the 1950's. Only a few were sold. Later a single-seat racing machine with its engine set crosswise was built. It, too, was unsuccessful.

Bugattis are perhaps the most desired of all vintage cars. Good ones meticulously restored (and overrestored) cost their weight in gold. And they're worth it!

1927 Type 41 Bugatti "Royale" Berline de Voyage.
Of saurian proportions, it had a 169-inch wheelbase and
a 13-liter engine that developed 300 hp; 125 mph
was possible. Built for kings, no monarch ever bought
one, despite its bargain price of $30,000.
Only six of the type exist.

Mercedes-Benz

The antecedents of Daimler-Benz Aktiengesellschaft, builders of the Mercedes-Benz, go farther back into the Stone Age of motoring than those of any other make. Gottlieb Daimler and Karl Benz did not, certainly, invent the automobile. But they were the first to make such a gasoline-engined device work with some reliability and regularity. And Karl Benz was the first man to produce self-propelled motor carriages for sale.

Gottlieb Daimler became interested in using gasoline to power small portable engines when he was only twenty-three and a student at Stuttgart's Polytechnic Institute. Benzine (we'd call the stuff gasoline today) had been discovered in 1825 by Michael Faraday and the dangerously inflammable stuff wasn't much used except in dry cleaning.

Before going to the Polytechnic, Daimler, not unlike Henry Royce and Mark Birkigt, had worked in a locomotive-building shop. In 1859 he returned to the shop after leaving the Polytechnic and tried to convince his boss that they ought to experiment with a benzine-powered engine. Understandably, he was unsuccessful. They'd stick to the old reliable steam engine, thank you.

In 1860, in Paris, Etienne Lenoir had built the first practical gas engine fueled by illuminating gas. In a French publication that Daimler came across, Lenoir had speculated that liquid fuel like benzine might also work. Daimler hied himself to Paris to see Lenoir and his huge crude engine. He was unimpressed, and he told Lenoir so.

After a couple of years in a steam-engine factory in England, Daimler came back to Germany, where he tried in vain to interest various people he worked for in his gasoline-engine ideas. Nor did he fare much better when he got a job at the Deutz Gasmotorenfabrik, where stationary illuminating-gas engines were being built. These were huge, slow-revving four-cycle, stationary engines used to power machinery in factories. Daimler made many improvements in the big engines during his ten years at Deutz, but he had to quit and set up his own workshop at Canstatt before he could devote himself to building his small, fast-revving, gasoline-powered engines. From Deutz he took with him his friend Wilhelm Maybach, who would make great contributions, especially with his improvements in the carburetor.

Late in 1883, Daimler at last got a patent on an engine with hot-tube ignition that would rev at the then unheard-of speed of 750 rpm. Daimler offered this engine, which weighed only 88 pounds per horsepower, to Deutz, whose big cooking-gas engines had top revs of 180 and weighed 725 pounds. But Deutz couldn't see any advantage in a portable engine that didn't have to be piped to a gasworks.

To prove the portability of his engine, Daimler installed one in a crude wooden bicycle he had built. But though the bike had

Preceding pages: 1927 Mercedes-Benz Model S with convertible cabriolet body by Saoutchik. The supercharged 6.8-liter, six-cylinder engine developed 120 hp without the supercharger and 180 hp with the blower engaged. Designed by Ferdinand Porsche, it was the forerunner of the more powerful SS models.

two wheels of the same size, unlike the then more common "penny-farthing" types with their huge front wheels, it was not too manageable. Daimler then installed one of his engines in a horse-carriage. But that motorized carriage was not the first to go pop-popping down a German road. Karl Benz had beaten Daimler to it, driving his three-wheeler on a public road in 1886.

Daimler was less interested in motorcars than he was in promoting his engines. He put them into motorboats, streetcars, even into an early airship. Certainly, he improved the cars he built. By 1889 he and Maybach had abandoned the motorized horse-carriage and exhibited a four-wheeled machine whose front end looked like a pair of bicycles, steering forks and all. It was powered by a two-cylinder V-engine with hot-tube ignition.

Hot-tube ignition needs a bit of explaining. Today an electric spark fires the gas-air charge in the cylinder. Daimler used no electricity. He depended on a small platinum tube screwed into the side of the cylinder, near the top. A burner fed by its own small tank of gasoline brought this tube to red heat. When the rising piston forced the compressed gas-air mixture into the hot tube, the mixture ignited. This primitive method worked surprisingly well, but it had serious drawbacks. The burners tended to be blown out by the wind, and in case of upset there was the danger of the burners setting spilled gas alight and incinerating the car.

It was not Daimler's cars but his engines, exported and licensed abroad, mostly to France, that gave automobilism its impetus in the very early days of the art.

Karl Benz, born in 1844 in Karlsruhe, Germany, had a much rougher time of it than Gottlieb Daimler. He and his widowed mother lived in grinding poverty, although he was able to get a fair education. (Germany was, in those days, ahead of most countries in offering schooling to the poor.) Benz attended the polytechnic school in Karlsruhe for four years. Afterward he struggled for years in various engineering shops, eventually starting a workshop of his own. He'd long been fascinated by gas engines and by 1878 was involved with a two-stroke engine of his own design.

Unlike Daimler, who had made a name for himself as an engineer with a big gas-engine company, Benz was continually in and out of financial difficulties with the small gas-engine companies he and various partners started. Sometimes the businesses just went bust. At other times his associates cheated him. But finally, with the backing of a couple of friends, he organized a company that worked—Benz und Cie., Rheinische Gasmotorenfabrik von Mannheim. This outfit was stable enough to allow Benz, late in 1883, to develop the engine *and* the car he had in mind. Benz had never seen a motorcar. He started from scratch, designing and building every bit of it himself—the frame, steering, transmission, engine.

The two-stroke stationary gas engines built by Benz und Cie. were too heavy for the car Benz envisioned. So he made a much

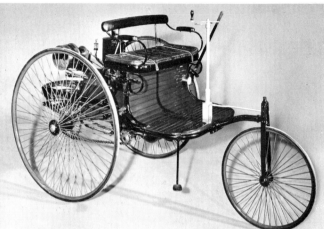

lighter four-stroke single-cylinder 8/10-hp engine. Like the stationary engines, it had electric ignition. The frame of that first Benz car was not unlike those of the pedal-propelled tricycles that were in vogue in the 1880's. But the tubing of which it was built was more robust in order to take the weight and the strains of the water-cooled engine and the belting and chains that transmitted power to the wire wheels.

Benz's engine lay aft, behind the two seats of his tricycle. Its single connecting rod projected nakedly from its horizontal cylinder and drove a big, spoked, horizontally disposed flywheel that the operator briskly pulled around to start the engine. Everything was exposed. There was no crankcase. Chains drove the rear axle, which had a differential. But a system of pulleys and a belt acted as a clutch before the chains were brought into action.

Benz started testing his motorized tricycle in the spring of 1885. That autumn it ran for a kilometer on the public highway at a speed of 12 kph. In 1886 Benz was driving it on the streets of Mannheim. But he drove secretly, late at night. Crowds and cops created too much of a fuss in the daytime. At first the car was depressingly unreliable and had to be pushed back to the shop time after time. But Benz continued to fuss with his *Motorwagen.*

Although his car became better and better, Benz's neglected gas-engine business became worse and worse, and his partners were most unhappy about his fiddling with the *Motorwagen.* His wife, however, remained staunchly enthusiastic. Each night when Herr Benz brought home the discharged battery that supplied the current for ignition, Frau Benz recharged it by means of a generator hooked up to the treadle of her sewing machine. She pumped away far into the night as Karl pondered drawings of improvements to his car.

It was Frau Benz who in 1888 went on the world's first long trip in a motorcar. At dawn one morning, while her spouse still lay abed, she and the two eldest Benz boys, fourteen and fifteen years old, climbed aboard the car. With Eugen Benz steering, they drove from Mannheim to Pforzheim. They had to dismount and push the little beast up every hill. But they made it. They made the return trip several days later. The first person to succeed in making a lengthy town-to-town journey in a wheeled vehicle without benefit of a horse was a middle-aged *Hausfrau.* And Benz learned that he needed a lower gear if his car was to make it up hills.

Encouraged by his wife's adventure, Benz drove his *"Patent-Motorwagen"* to the great fair at Munich—a 200-mile jaunt. He caused a lot of excitement and won the gold medal. The publicity was gratifying, but sales were not. At the Paris Exposition of 1889 (where the new Eiffel Tower was the main attraction) Benz had somewhat better luck. Emile Roger, a French bicycle builder, bought a Benz car and set up a French distributorship. He named the car the Roger-Benz and managed to sell a few. But Benz's partners had had enough. They pulled out of the company.

Top left: First advertisement for the Benz three-wheeler appeared in 1888. Top right: 1886 Benz "Patent-Motorwagen." Bottom left: Herr Emile Jellinek and his daughter Mercedes, after whom the Mercedes car was named. Bottom right: The car in this poster looks like a 1912–1914 model.

Two new men came into the picture: F. Von Fischer and Julius Ganss. Ganss, the salesman of the pair, was soon selling Benz cars all over Europe. These were still three-wheelers, but by 1892 Benz had a four-wheeled machine ready. In 1897 two-cylinder Benzes were produced. Within a few years Benz was selling hundreds of cars of various sizes and models. He could hardly keep up with the demand. But he was a stubborn old Teuton. While other makers of cars, notably in France, were forging ahead, Benz stuck to his slow-speed engines, his belts, and his chains.

By 1902 the Benz company was in poor shape. First, an engineer, Marius Barbarou, was brought over from France. He and a gang of Frenchmen designed and built a shaft-driven car, the Benz Parsifal. This was a dud. Karl Benz and his son Eugen quit the company. Then Ganss quit. Then Barbarou, in a huff, left for France. Finally, Benz came back and made the Parsifal into a so-so machine.

But enough of Benz. What made the name Mercedes-Benz a great one was the Mercedes, not the Benz. True, the Benz had to some extent been successful in pre-World War I racing, and the Blitzen Benzes raced by Barney Oldfield and by Bob Burman, who broke the world's land speed record in one in 1911, were very famous indeed. But if it hadn't been for the Daimler-built Mercedes, the Benz would be remembered mostly because it was, in 1886, the first successful car. That, of course, is quite something.

The first Mercedes was designed by Gottlieb Daimler's old friend Wilhelm Maybach in 1900. By then Herr Daimler was much too ill with heart trouble to take an active part in his company, and his son Paul and Maybach pretty much ran things. The car was named Mercedes after the young daughter of one Emile Jellinek, a busy little wheeler-dealer who was at the time the Austro-Hungarian consul in Nice and a director of the Crédit-Lyonnais, a French bank. Among Jellinek's pals on the then very fancy Côte d'Azur were various English dukes, Russian princes, and American millionaires who found nesting places in the south of France each winter. He made himself a tidy sum by selling them Daimler cars, for which he was a sort of unofficial agent.

It was fashionable at the time to indulge in the new sport of motor racing. When the superrich weren't trying to kill themselves steeplechasing or slaughtering pigeons with shotguns in Monte Carlo, they toyed with automobiles. To keep up with his gilded friends, Jellinek also went motor racing. And like them he stylishly hid behind a pseudonym. (It was not *au fait* to have your real name printed in a racing program.) Jellinek chose his daughter's name, Mercedes.

In 1899 Jellinek had tried driving a new Canstatt-Daimler racing machine. This 28-hp monster was a heavy little brute, high and with a ridiculously short wheelb.. . It was almost unsteerable and unstoppable, and it was exceedingly dangerous. Wilhelm Bauer, fore-

Top left: 1892 Benz single-cylinder engine.
Top right: 1885 Daimler 1 1/2-hp single-cylinder engine.
Middle: The first Mercedes of 1900 started a
revolution in car design. Bottom: The 1899 Daimler-Phoenix
had four cylinders, was too short, too high,
and remarkably dangerous to drive.

man of the Daimler factory, was killed by one of them before Jellinek got his turn behind the wheel.

Jellinek was, understandably, terrified by that Canstatt-Daimler and took himself off to the factory to tell Paul Daimler and Wilhelm Maybach what he thought of their racing machine. He also had enough chutzpa to tell them what kind of machine they ought to be building. And since he sold so many expensive Daimlers to his expensive friends, he had enough clout to get away with it.

The new car immediately made every other automobile in the wold obsolete.

Longer and lower, it looked unlike any other car in existence in 1900. For decades afterward, all other touring cars would merely be developments of its shape. Up front was a honeycomb radiator mounted in a way that would be common almost until our time. Its four-cylinder 5.32-liter engine, which developed 35 hp at 1,000 rpm, had mechanically opened inlet valves that allowed speed control by means of a throttle. "Automatic" inlet valves of other car engines were still opened by the suction of descending pistons. Such valves forced an engine to run at an almost constant speed, and the only way to change a car's speed was to shift gears. Ignition was by a new Simms-Bosch low-tension magneto. "Make-and-break" switches inside the cylinders created a spark as they opened and thus fired the gas-air charge. The gearshift, for the first time, operated in a "gate." The rear-wheel brakes were internally expand-

ing—another innovation. And the chassis frame was of pressed steel at a time when most cars still used wood reinforced with flitch plates.

Jellinek was mightily impressed by the new car while it was still under construction and in April, 1900, he grandiloquently ordered thirty-six of them to be delivered to him within six months. Further, he insisted that the car bear the name "Mercedes."

When word of the big doings at the Daimler factory got around, other manufacturers started biting their nails. But they breathed sighs of relief when the new Mercedes got its first test. Jellinek had made the factory so nervous with his continual hurry-up tactics that it sent the unprepared and untested new car by railway from Canstatt to Paris. There it failed miserably, stripping its gears and ruining its bearings. Shipped by train again to Pau for its maiden Grand Prix, where it was driven by Lorraine Barrow (who later died in the 1903 Paris-Madrid), it again misbehaved. Its clutch slipped and the gear-changing lever refused to change gears. Barrow quit after about 15 feet.

But the new Mercedes was merely having teething troubles. After the mechanics from Canstatt got down to work on it, the revolutionary new car showed what it could do in the Nice-Salon-Nice race over the Alpes Maritimes in March, 1901. Driven by Wilhelm Werner, it outran everything else with its 36.63-mph average for the 279.45 miles.

That first Mercedes was a mere pussycat, though, compared with the Mercedes

Top: This 1904 28-hp, four-cylinder Mercedes-Simplex had an American-built body. Bottom: The 1927 Mercedes-Benz Model K had a six-cylinder, 6.2-liter supercharged engine that developed 110 hp without the blower, about 150 hp mit kompressor. Although the K is rather a brute to drive, collectors love it.

Sixty of 1903. Seventy-five years ago the difference between a racing car and a car that might be used on the road was rather blurred. And the kind of rakish young superrich sport who today must have nothing less potent than a 180-mph Ferrari Boxer, in 1903 just had to be seen—and heard—in a Mercedes Sixty that cost Papa some $12,000—about $120,000 in our debased currency. If fitted with a pair of huge brass acetylene headlamps and plowsharelike fenders, the Sixty was a sports car. (The term was unknown in 1903.) Stripped, it was a racing car.

It was in just such a slightly undressed Sixty that the fierce, red-bearded Camille Jenatzy won the 1903 Gordon Bennett race in Ireland.

It had not been the Canstatt factory's intention to run Sixties in that race. Six monstrous 90-hp Mercedes had been prepared to run, but a fire had destroyed not only the factory but also five of the Nineties. There was nothing to do but run three Sixties, which were nearly as fast. But the factory had only two Sixties. So one was borrowed from an American millionaire, Clarence Gray Dinsmore, stripped of its road equipment, and handed to Jenatzy. The other Sixties were driven by Foxhall-Keene and the Baron de Caters. Both retired with broken rear axles. Jenatzy won the 327½-mile race by twelve minutes over De Knyff's 80-hp Panhard, which came in second. Jenatzy averaged 55.3 mph, very fast indeed in 1903.

Today we would consider the four-cylinder, 9¼-liter engine of the Sixty very large.

But in its day it was, compared with engines of 14 to 18 liters like those in Panhards and Mors, a mere stripling. Ignition was from a low-tension magneto that fed current to make-and-break switches inside the cylinders.

Controlling engine speed by means of a throttle on the carburetor was still not entirely practical in 1903. Instead of a foot-controlled throttle on the carburetor, the inlet valves' lift could be varied by means of a wildly complex system of rods, pinions, toothed racks, and whatnot, controlled from "a handle on the steering wheel . . . [that] varies the quantity of explosive mixture drawn into the cylinders." (The quotation is from A. B. Filson Young's 1904 book, *The Complete Motorist*.) Valve timing could also be controlled. Such control of engine speed was unusual in 1903, when most engines ran at an almost constant speed. But don't imagine that a Sixty's engine was anywhere near as controllable for downshifting as a modern engine, for it developed its peak power at only 1,000 rpm.

A "scroll" clutch, a helical spring that grabbed the drive shaft in a boa-constrictor-like death grip, transmitted power to a four-speed gearbox, which, in turn, drove the double chains to the rear wheels. The internal expanding metal-to-metal two-wheel brakes received a shot of cooling water at each application. This cooling of the brake drums was as innovative as the fact that the brakes were internally expanding. Twenty-five years later, a 1928 Buick I used to ride in still had externally contracting brakes.

No one today really knows what it was like to drive a Sixty in 1903. For over the years the few that survived were so modified and "improved" that the joys of things like variable-lift valves and even make-and-break ignition could no longer be experienced.

But we do know that the Mercedes Sixty intoxicated its drivers with a feeling of omnipotence. And a fair number of young heirs to millions didn't live to collect their inheritances after trying to find out how fast they could negotiate a twisting Alpine road. For although a Sixty could reach 85 mph, it still had 1903 steering—about one turn lock-to-lock—and two-wheel brakes that turned their cooling water into instant steam.

For the next decade or so, until after the Kaiser War, most Mercedes and Benz passenger cars were well engineered and constructed. They were admirably durable but decidedly dull.

After Versailles, the German economy was in ruins. Inflation almost put both Benz and Mercedes out of business, and it became obvious to the directors of both companies that a merger was the best means for survival. In May, 1924, they signed an "Agreement of Mutual Interest" that contained a clause guaranteeing Karl and Berta Benz financial security for the rest of their lives. In June, 1926, the new firm of Daimler-Benz Aktiengesellschaft came into being.

Karl Benz died on April 4, 1929, aged eighty-five. Frau Benz, who had bravely taken that first long drive in a motorcar in 1888, died in 1944, when she was ninety-five.

It wasn't until the late 1920's that Mercedes-Benz again built sporting motorcars that could raise the blood pressure of autophiles as the Sixty had done twenty-odd years earlier. The first of these machines that I, in my youth, became aware of was a Mercedes-Benz K, or 33/180.

Fifty years ago I was the lowliest staff member in the New York art department of a big movie company. The star of the department was a flamboyant gentleman who not only painted lush posters extolling such ladies as Joan Crawford and Greta Garbo, but also painted equine portraits for his horsey socialite friends on Long Island's gold coast. To commute from Long Island to the Times Square building where we worked, the artist used a white-painted, open, K Mercedes-Benz. He never drove but sat up front beside his chauffeur, whom he had decked out in a white livery. The owner also dragged an expensive white leather overcoat along the ground as he strode from the Mercedes to the building.

His performance with the white coat certainly impressed me (although the coat became less white after several weeks), but it was the car that really held my attention (as well as that of a small crowd of onlookers). It was a veritable locomotive of a machine with a pointed radiator and an impossibly long hood from which curled huge nickel-plated exhaust pipes. The body sides were cut away to show the white

leather seats, and the instrument panel exhibited a formidable array of mysterious dials. But best of all was the ground-shaking rumble as the chauffeur took off after his master had left.

Although the owner of the Mercedes-Benz sat not ten feet away from me as he drew his improbably perfect movie queens, I never got up enough nerve to ask him for a ride. And then one day he announced: "I've just traded my car for two tin-can American cars, Auburns. That Mercedes attracted too much attention."

For a long time I dreamed about that big Mercedes-Benz as the unattainably perfect machine that I might someday own.

Above: English-bodied 1910 four-cylinder chain-drive Mercedes. Top right: Poster of the late 1930's. Far right: Front view of the 1904 Mercedes-Simplex and its engine, which originally had "make-and-break" ignition but has been converted to more modern magneto ignition. Right: Bold prow of the 1927 Mercedes-Benz S.

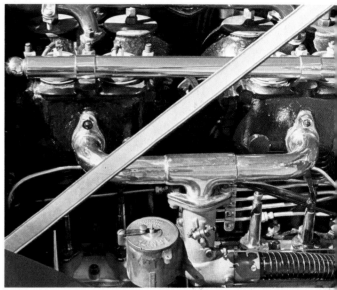

When I at last became familiar with a K, I changed my mind. In about 1931 a friend of mine bought one for a few hundred dollars, for the Depression had quickly made such cars very cheap. I soon learned to fear that car.

The K had first appeared in 1926, the year Mercedes had married Benz, and it was one of the first fruits of that union. It was designed by Ferdinand Porsche, who had been with Austro-Daimler and had joined Mercedes in 1923. Later he was responsible for the rear-engined Auto-Union Grand Prix cars, the Wehrmacht's huge Tiger tank, and the Volkswagen.

The K had a six-cylinder 6.2-liter engine with a single overhead camshaft, and it was supercharged. Hence K for *Kompressor*. A top speed of 100 mph was claimed. That engine was a joy to contemplate, for it displayed the kind of Germanically intense devotion to detail that no longer exists, even on today's most expensive automobiles.

My friend's K, luckily, would not reach 100 mph, for its roadholding abilities were not equal to such rapid progression. I was terrified as I sat beside its driver at even 70 mph. For at that modest speed, on a straight stretch, it needed the whole width of a two-lane road as it bounced and swayed from side to side. You can imagine the trauma of cornering. That K's brakes were not the best, either. They were, I must admit, better than the two-wheel brakes on my late 1908 Welch. But they weren't much better.

Brave people *did* reach 90 mph on K's. And Rudolf Caracciola, who was *very* brave, set a flying-kilometer sports-car record at Freiburg in 1926 by driving a K at 95 mph.

Within a year Ferdinand Porsche transformed the K into one of the most desirable sporting machines of all time. The new S, or 36-220, Mercedes-Benz had none of the vices of the old K and it had virtues that perhaps only one other car of 1927 could equal—the Type 43 Bugatti, an entirely different kind of animal. The S was a big car, with a very big supercharged engine of 6.8 liters—over twice as big as that of the Bugatti. Without its blower, the S had 120 bhp (at 3,000 rpm) at its disposal. With its *kompressor* in use, 180 bhp was developed. Superchargers were not uncommon in 1927, but the one on the S Mercedes worked only when you wanted it to. Other cars' blowers ran all the time. When you stamped on the S's accelerator a clutch engaged the supercharger and the extra 60 horsepower caused the car to leap ahead as a howling, screaming wail joined the usual high-speed roar from its exhaust. The Luftwaffe's Stukas of a decade or so later had nothing on an S with its blower in action.

The wail from a blown S was due to the way the Roots-type *kompressor* blew air through its twin Pallas carburetors. Other cars' superchargers sucked mixture from their carburetors before compressing it and pushing it into the cylinders. Owners were cautioned against using their *kompressors* too exuberantly: never for more than twenty seconds while ac-

Top: The 1937 Type W 125 5.6-liter, eight-cylinder Mercedes Benz Grand Prix machine developed almost 650 hp. Middle left: 1914 Grand Prix Mercedes. Middle right: 1938-1940 V-12 Type 154 3-liter, 450-hp supercharged Grand Prix Mercedes-Benz engine. Bottom: 1931 supercharged Mercedes-Benz SSKL could exceed 150 mph.

celerating, never in top gear at top speed nor from rest in low gear.

An S Mercedes-Benz with an open four-passenger body could slightly exceed 100 mph. But unlike the K, it had excellent road manners, adequate brakes, and fairly light steering when under way, if not at parking speeds. Finish and precision of construction were not one whit inferior to those of the Bugatti or Alfa Romeo.

In 1928 the S became the 38/250 SS, which had a slightly larger engine—7 liters. Its compression ratio was slightly greater at 7 to 1, and more power was produced—170 bhp without the blower engaged. *Mit kompressor* it increased to 225 bhp. The shorter, lighter SSK's (K for *kurz,* "short") *kompressor* blew a bit harder and its engine put out 250 bhp.

Porsche left Mercedes-Benz in 1928 and Hans Nibel, who had designed the old Blitzen Benz, took over development of the SSK.

At the Nürburgring in 1928, Caracciola showed what he could do with an SS against a swarm of agile Grand Prix Bugattis at a time when Ettore's cars still had things their own way in racing. "Carratsch" came in first. Two other SS's took second and third places. It is hard to think of a less suitable car than a big SSK for the curly course of the Monaco Grand Prix through the streets of Monte Carlo. But in 1929 Caracciola actually tried it and was only two minutes and thirteen seconds from winning against the countless Bugattis. Tire trouble put him in third place.

The SSKL's (L for *leicht,* "light") were developed for racing. Private owners were not supposed to be able to buy them. But one evening in the late 1930's I was much amazed when one screamed past me on New York's Sixth Avenue. Its driver stopped for a traffic light and I drew up next to the SSKL in my 1,750-cc Alfa. It was an SSKL, all right, with saucer-sized lightening holes drilled in its chassis frame. I couldn't, however, quite see who was driving it, for although it was a two-seater, its driver was almost hidden by what seemed like at least four spectacular chorus-girl types whom he'd somehow sardined aboard. Seeing me in the Alfa, he took off with his foot down hard on the gas (which was strictly *verboten* by the factory). Other traffic took quick evading action to get clear of what was obviously a fire engine with an especially loud siren.

An SSKL with an oversized "elephant" blower was said to devlop some 300 bhp. Driving an SSKL in the 1931 Italian Mille Miglia, which comprised 1,000 miles of rough mountain roads in a great figure-eight from Brescia to Rome and back, Caracciola won over a howling pack of Alfa Romeos and a couple of O.M.'s. On the 129-mile stretch between Brescia and Bologna, "Carratsch" *averaged* 95.8 mph. Remember, this was close to fifty years ago!

In that same year, Caracciola in an SSKL also won the German Grand Prix at the Nürburgring against two Type 51 Bugattis driven by Louis Chiron and Achille Varzi, and an Alfa Romeo driven by Tazio Nuvolari.

Preceding pages: 1956 300 SL "gull-wing"
Mercedes-Benz has a 3-liter fuel-injected six-cylinder
engine that develops 240 hp. Almost 150 mph
is possible, and zero to 60 mph takes about eight
seconds. Gull-wing models cost only some $7,500 in their day
and are now worth more than five times that.

During the Hitler years, Mercedes-Benz, subsidized by the Nazis for the greater glory of the Third Reich, was well-nigh unbeatable in Grand Prix racing. Only Ferdinand Porsche's Auto-Unions, which were also the recipients of Hitler's largesse, gave the Mercedes-Benzes any trouble.

But the years of national socialism saw the end of the great Mercedes S-types. The most notable machines of those dark times were the obese and blowsy 500 K's and 540 K's. Curvilinear and swoopy-fendered, they still delight the collectors who love Auburn Speedsters.

The 5-liter supercharged eight-cylinder engine of the 500 K, with pushrod-operated valves, had its work cut out for it in propelling the 5,000-pound car. In top gear with its blower engaged, not much over 100 mph was possible. Without the supercharger only 85 or so was attainable. In third gear only 60 mph could be reached before valve bounce set in. Using the blower, zero to 60 mph took about sixteen seconds. The slightly more powerful (and even heavier) 540 K could reach 106 mph with its supercharger in action. In third gear 75 mph could be reached and zero to 60 took fourteen seconds. With its blower clutched in a 540 K developed 180 bhp; sans blower, 115.

A 540 K cost over $10,000 in New York in the late 1930's. Misguided collectors pay five times that today.

When World War II ended, the Daimler-Benz factories, which had been prime targets of British and American bombers,

weren't much more than holes in the ground. But within a few years Mercedes-Benz cars were out there winning Grand Prix and sports-car races. And Daimler-Benz's passenger cars were soon selling better than ever, especially to stock-broker types who quickly embraced them as status symbols. Most of the multifarious production cars were rather forgettable albeit well made and more than normally reliable.

A few of the cars stand out from the ruck. The 300 SL, for example (SL for *super leicht*). The 300 SL competition sports car prototype was first unveiled early in 1951. A year later, in May, 1952, three 300 SL's ran in the Italian Mille Miglia. One of them, driven by Karl Kling, came in second. A month later two 300 SL's took first and second places in the Le Mans twenty-four-hour race. In November, 1952, Karl Kling won the grueling 1,934-mile Carrera Panamericana, which traversed the full length of Mexico, at an average speed of 102.59 mph. And so it went. Victories piled up.

The Mercedes-Benz distributor in the United States soon suggested that a sports car similar to the competition 300 SL be put into production for sale to the public. By 1955 you could walk into a showroom and buy one.

The production model of the 300 SL had a single-overhead-camshaft 3-liter six-cylinder engine. The competition machines' engines had had carburetors, but the new cars' engines had fuel injection. Compression ratio was 8.55 to 1, and 240 bhp was developed at 5,800 rpm. A dry sump lubrication system was standard. It was a beautifully flexible engine and the car could be driven in top gear at 25 mph and then taken right up to its top speed of almost 150 mph. Zero to 60 took about eight seconds. A four-speed synchromesh gearbox was fitted. Suspension was by coil springs with swing-axles aft. The huge servo-boosted Al-Fin brakes were just so-so at top speed. The later roadster models had discs. The machinery was hung from a beautifully light space frame of steel tubing that weighed only 180 pounds. The whole gull-winged car was only some 2,700 pounds.

A friend of mine owned an early 300 SL in the late 1950's, and I once managed to really terrify myself in it. On the straight at high speed it handled splendidly. It cornered beautifully, though with more than a hint of oversteer. But I got a bit too exuberant on a corner and without warning its tail swung out and I lost it. I'd never known a car (except for a low-chassis Invicta I once owned) that behaved so viciously so suddenly. Luckily, I failed to bend that beautiful 300 SL. The car's Achilles heel was, of course, its rear swing-axles. The later roadster model was much less of an oversteerer and had better manners on corners.

The first gull-wing 300 SL's cost about $7,500 in New York in the late 1950's. You'd need over $40,000 to buy a good one these days.

The super-Mercedes-Benz of the mid-1960's (it first appeared in 1963) was the vast and luxurious 600. In the class of the Rolls-Royce, it made the Silver Shadow look like a compact. In long-chassis form it had three doors on each flank and a veritable club room aft for its pampered inmates. Although it weighed not much less than 6,000 pounds it handled like a sports car and was claimed to reach 125 mph from its 300 bhp. Very boring. But Arab billionaires who could pack it full of wives loved it. Its $30,000-plus pre-double-digit-inflation price tag meant nothing to them.

The hottest Mercedes-Benz around today is the 450 SEL 6.9, which when I last looked cost $38,230 laid down in New York. It is the fastest four-door sedan you can buy today. Its fuel-injected, dry sump, single-overhead-camshaft V-8 6,834-cc engine churns out 250 bhp at 4,000 rpm, giving the 6.9 a top speed of over 130 mph and a zero-to-60 time of eight seconds. And at 4,390 pounds, the 6.9 is far from being a lightweight.

But it is the spectacular manner of its going that makes the admittedly complex 6.9 unique. Its sophisticated self-leveling hydro-pneumatic suspension (not too unlike that on the Citroën) makes its speed safe and comfortable on roads that lesser cars' drivers must negotiate with circumspection.

During the past three-quarters of a century Daimler-Benz has come up with three super-Mercedes: the Sixty of 1903, the S of 1927, and the 300 SL of 1952. About a quarter of a century went by between each of them. Some twenty-five years have now passed since the days of the 300 SL. Is it about time for a new super-Mercedes?

Top: Superluxury Mercedes-Benz 600 first appeared in 1963. The boardroom-size rear was almost big enough to hold an oil-company directorate plus Arab friends. Bottom: Special 6.9-liter version of the 450 SEL is the fastest four-door sedan you can buy— 130 mph and zero to 60 mph in eight seconds.

Ferrari is a magic name. It conjures up visions of super speed and wonderful noises. It is the car lusted after by speed-loving young men but bought mostly by the very rich middle-aged. The Ferrari is the Bugatti of our time and the true descendant of the great Alfa Romeos of the 1930's. As the Bugatti was the artistic expression of that eccentric Italian genius Ettore Bugatti, so the Ferrari is the result of the single-mindedness of another very tough Italian, Enzo Ferrari.

Enzo Ferrari was no artist in metal as was Bugatti. He sat at no drawing board penciling revolutionary ideas for camshafts and axles; his engineers have always done that. But Ferrari knew and got exactly what he demanded from them.

Enzo Ferrari was born near Modena in 1898. His father owned a shop that made structural metalwork for the Italian State Railways. The family lived upstairs, over the noisy workshop. Evidently they had enough money to further his father's wish that Enzo become an engineer. But Enzo was no scholar. He hated school. He wanted to pursue one of the occupations beloved by so many young Italian romantics—opera singing or race driving. His ambition to be a racing-car driver was traceable at least in part to the time his father took him and his brother Alfredo to a race at Bologna. There the young Ferrari saw those *artistes* of automobile racing, Felice Nazzaro and Vincenzo Lancia

(who also had had operatic ambitions), driving huge Fiats.

In 1916 things came apart for Enzo Ferrari. His father and his brother Alfredo died—his father at home of pneumonia and his brother in a military hospital. Enzo was eighteen and adrift. In 1917 the hard-pressed Italian army grabbed him. There he too became very sick and the army doctors gave him up as incurable. He surprised them, got better, and was mustered out.

There were few jobs for the discharged soldiers of Italy's army, but Ferrari was luckier than most. He was hired as a driver by a fellow who was rebuilding old Lancia army trucks into passenger cars. After the truck chassis were converted into passenger-car chassis, Enzo drove them to Milan to be fitted with passenger-car bodies. He wasn't yet a race-car driver, but at least he was driving for pay. And he made enough money to hang out in the bars frequented by real racing drivers.

One of the drivers with whom he became friendly was Ugo Sivocci, a test driver for C.M.N. (Costruzioni Meccaniche Nazionali), a long-gone make. Sivocci was also in charge of the firm's racing and got Ferrari a job as his assistant. Suddenly Ferrari was a racing driver. He came in ninth in the 1919 Targa Florio and third in a very obscure hill climb.

This experience got him a job a year later as a test driver for Alfa Romeo, which was back building cars after years of turning out military equipment. In turn, Enzo got Ugo a

*Preceding pages: 1949 Type 166 Mille Miglia
was the factory's first production car. Called the
Barchetta—"Little Boat"—it had a V-12, 2-liter, 140-hp
engine. Body was by Carrozzeria Touring. Luigi
Chinetti, with Lord Selsdon as codriver, won the 24-hour race
at Le Mans in 1949 in a similar machine.*

job as chief test driver for Alfa. In those days it was common for some test drivers to become factory-team racing drivers. Ferrari at last had his chance to drive for a firm that would soon field some of the greatest racing cars and drivers of all time.

But Ferrari never became a great driver. True, he placed in the Targa Florio a few times in the early 1920's. But his later exploits were in obscure local races and hill climbs.

Still, Ferrari must in those days have been a most likable and bright young fellow. He was also a shrewd climber and soon made himself indispensable to Giorgio Rimini, the sales manager, who, since racing was part of sales promotion, was also in charge of Alfa Romeo's racing program.

In those days Alfa's chief engineer was Giuseppe Merosi, who had designed the tough, fast, and successful RL and RL Super Sport models as well as the racing RLTF Targa Florio cars, one of which Ferrari drove in that race without success. In the early twenties, the Fiat racing stable was well-nigh unbeatable. Merosi had designed a racing Alfa Romeo, the P1, to challenge Fiat, but the resulting machine was somewhat disappointing. Ferrari had a friend in Fiat's racing department, Luigi Bazzi, and he talked him into coming to work for Alfa Romeo. At Alfa, Bazzi was put to work improving the P1. He also told the Alfa people about a great young engineer who was working at Fiat, Vittorio Jano. Jano, he said, was just the man to design a new car to beat the Fiats.

Nicola Romeo, Alfa's head man, agreed, and Ferrari was sent to lure Jano away from Fiat. He was empowered to offer Jano a big raise in pay, a free hand in designing, and even the opportunity to run the Alfa Romeo racing team. But Jano would deal with no underling. Giorgio Rimini himself had to journey to Turin to close the deal in September, 1923.

Vittorio Jano was the best thing that ever happened to Alfa Romeo. In the end it was he who made the name great. One of the greatest automotive engineers in history, he designed not only the successful P2 and P3 racing machines, but also the wonderful Alfa Romeo sports cars, the great 1750's and 2.3's. The present-day Ferrari is directly descended from his work and from the designs of his protégé, Gioacchino Colombo, who came to Alfa Romeo in 1924.

The P2's trounced the Fiats, the Bugattis, and everything else in 1924 and 1925. But in 1925 Alfa quit Grand Prix racing after the death of its top driver, Antonio Ascari, in the French Grand Prix. Although Alfa claimed that it had withdrawn from racing out of respect for its fallen hero, another reason perhaps was the fact that it had been taken over by the Italian government to forestall its bankruptcy. The bureaucrats may not have been too crazy about the tremendously costly Grand Prix racing program. Sports-car racing, however, still went on.

Enzo Ferrari, despite the lull in Grand Prix racing, was for a time deeply involved in promoting and selling the delectable

*Top left: Closed version of a Barchetta by Touring
at the Bridgehampton, Long Island, races in the early 1950's.
Bottom left: 1967 330 GTC Ferrari. Top right: 365 GTB/4
Daytona has a V-12, 4 1/2-liter engine and is
capable of 175 mph. Bottom right: 1958 2 1/2-liter, V-6,
Dino-engined Formula One Grand Prix Ferrari.*

Alfa Romeo sports cars. He cultivated the rich sports-car owners and acted as a sort of liaison man between them and the factory. In 1929, with the backing of some of the rich people he'd made friends with, he formed the Scuderia Ferrari in Modena under the aegis of the Alfa factory. It was a sort of dummy outfit that not only sold and maintained racing cars, but also took charge of Alfa Romeo racing activities. It was quite successful until Hitler's Mercedes-Benz and Auto-Union cars began to regularly defeat Mussolini's Alfas.

In 1938 Alfa took over its own racing program again under the name of Alfa Corse with Ferrari at its head. By now Alfa had pretty much given up trying to compete with the Germans in Formula One racing and was campaigning the Alfetta, the Colombo-designed 1,500-cc Type 158/59, in *voiturette* racing.

There was a Spanish engineer named Wilfredo Ricart (he later designed the Pegaso), who worked for Alfa Corse and whom Ferrari detested. In 1939 Ferrari got into a hassle with Alfa's managing director, Ugo Gobbato, over Ricart's undue influence in the design department. Ferrari quit his job with Alfa. Now he was free to build his own car. But he had earlier agreed with Alfa that if he ever left, he wouldn't put his own name on a car for four years.

Ferrari still owned the premises in Modena, had saved money over the years, and had some rich friends with money to invest. He formed a company, the Societa Auto-Avio Costruzione, which at first did some subcontracting for an airplane-engine builder. Then, with the help of Enrico Nardi and other friends, he built two 1,500-cc cars. For the shortened 1940 Mille Miglia (called the Gran Premio di Brescia) they weren't called Ferraris. They were known simply as Vettura 815's and had a lot of Fiat under their skins. Both cars were unsuccessful.

During the Hitler War Ferrari made himself a nice little pile building machine tools for war production, both at Modena and in a new factory at Maranello. After the war, despite having received the titles of *Commendatore* and *Cavaliere* from the Mussolini government, Enzo seems to have avoided reprisals. Neither did Colombo suffer much for having been an enthusiastic Fascist.

In 1946 Colombo started to design the first Ferrari, a V-12 1,500-cc machine, the Tipo 125. (The number 125, as in almost all later Ferraris, indicated the cubic capacity of the individual cylinders.) V-12 engines were nothing new to Colombo. The big prewar Grand Prix Alfas of the late 1930's had been V-12's. But somehow the engine design of the Tipo 125 wasn't quite right, perhaps because Colombo was too busy to devote all his time to it. He called in Aurelio Lampredi to replace him at the drawing board. The V-12 ohc engine he finally designed became the progenitor for practically every V-12 Ferrari engine ever built, except for the recent 365 GT/4 (the Boxer Berlinetta), whose cylinders are horizontally opposed, and the Dinos.

The engines of Ferrari Grand Prix

Top: Dr. Nino Farina nonchalantly conducts a Type 500 F2 four-cylinder Formula Two Grand Prix Ferrari in 1952. Bottom: Froilan Gonzalez driving the 5-liter, twelve-cylinder Ferrari sports car at the Le Mans 24-hour race in 1954. He and his partner, Maurice Trintignant, won.

cars have had other configurations. They've been fours, eights, sixes, as well as V-12's.

Lampredi left Ferrari in 1955. Since then a succession of other designers, including Colombo and Jano, have worked on the almost three hundred different engine types produced at Maranello since 1946. It seems that there must be that many different models of Ferrari car, too. I don't think that Enzo himself can possibly remember how many different kinds of Ferrari have borne his name and his prancing-horse blazon.

The first Ferrari I ever saw was the one George Rand drove at the Bridgehampton road race in 1949. It was the Type 166, with a cycle-fendered body that had been imported by Briggs Cunningham a few months earlier. It was the very first Ferrari to have arrived in the United States. I was much awed by the fantastic and delightful noises it made and by the sight of the twelve-cylinder engine under its hood. No postwar engine had such a delectable look and finish. But I do recollect being rather disappointed with the finish and construction of the chassis and running gear. Were it a Bugatti, I thought, the chassis would have been as beautiful as the engine. At first Rand just ran away from the oddly assorted cars in that first Bridgehampton—ancient Alfa Romeos, peculiar specials, superannuated Bugattis, and the tanklike 1940 Mille Miglia BMW driven by Bob Grier. Sadly, Rand's Ferrari broke an oil line and retired. I don't recall the car or the driver that won that delightful race through the Long Island potato fields.

After the Type 166 came a flood of Ferraris bought by rich men newly attracted to foreign sports cars. Earlier they had bought MG's, then XK 120 Jaguars. Now they just *had* to have the best that money could buy—Ferraris. And Alfred Momo's shop in Woodside, Queens, near Manhattan, suddenly seemed full of machines from Maranello. Soon Zumbach's in New York also learned how to repair some of the more fragile parts of the Ferraris' anatomies. For, engines apart, very early sports Ferraris did have some vulnerable components, some of which were more Fiat than Ferrari. Today the GT Ferraris you can buy off the showrooom floor are paragons of reliability, as tough as the the Formula One Ferraris that from the beginning have dominated the world's Grands Prix.

Until almost the mid-1950's Ferrari built few Gran Turismo machines in series. Such road cars as were produced for private owners all had special bodies, no two of which were alike. Almost all of the earlier Ferraris were near-competition cars, and some of them had very beautiful and even comfortably habitable coachwork.

North Italian *carrozzeristi* share with the Swiss and the south Germans an ancient tradition of sheet-metal working. They were the artisans who turned out the exquisite armor of the sixteenth century. And bashing out a steel breastplate or morion is not too different from hammering away at a fender or hood. Vignale,

Top: Chinetti NART 312 PB flat-12-engined sports-racing Ferrari that won the manufacturers' world championship in 1972. Middle: Driver's compartment of the 312 PB. Bottom: Elegantly styled 1978 308 GTS Ferrari has sting in its rear, where its V-8, 3-liter, 240-hp engine resides.

Bertone, Stabilimente Farina, Pininfarina, Boano, Ghia, "Superleggera" Touring, Scaglietti, Zagato, all of Turin and Milan, built bodies for Ferrari. In recent years some of them have been mass-producing the bodies they design, a felicitous Italian system that exists in no other country.

Such mass production has been used for some models of Alfa Romeos, Fiats, and Lancias. They have been built by the thousand. Ferrari, too, has been using such series production of bodies, but seldom in more than batches of a hundred or so, which makes it highly unlikely that you'll ever see a Ferrari resembling the one you're driving parked next to you anywhere in the world.

I've been driven in a fair number of Ferraris, starting with a little 1950-ish 166 Inter—a Barchetta. Then in a 212 Export or two, and even in a big tough 1956 4.1-liter Super America. I've driven a few Ferraris, too, among them a 1965 275 GTB Ferrari and a 365 GTB/4 Daytona. Amazingly, although the cars spanned about a quarter of a century, they all had that same very definable, very Italian Ferrari feel.

A Ferrari can have torque-tube drive or an open propeller shaft, a five-speed gearbox or a four-speed box, independent rear suspension or a solid rear axle, drum brakes or disc brakes. But a Ferrari still feels like a Ferrari, even with power steering and air conditioning.

Turn the ignition key and the twelve-cylinder engine literally explodes into action, instantly snarling, howling, roaring. You can almost feel your blood pressure rise, your adrenaline pump in unison with the oil pressure. Press down the firm but not too heavy clutch pedal, move the accurate-feeling gear lever into first—the machine moves and you instantly shift into second, then third; a touch of the gas pedal and the rev counter needle flies past the divisions on the scale, 3,000, 4,000. There's a corner ahead. The brakes—drums on the Barchetta, discs on a Daytona—retard you in exact relation to the pressure of your leg muscles. The steering reacts to the input from your wrists in the same way. Each tiny increment of pressure from your toe on the gas pedal makes a definite change in engine speed. You can play the varying sounds of the engine like some superaccurate musical instrument.

You reach an open stretch of road. In fourth speed you suddenly find yourself in the 90's. It feels like 50 in that American sedan you've been driving around town. And fifth

*Top left: 1954 Ferrari 375 MM built by
Pinin Farina for Ingrid Bergman but never delivered.
Left: Graham Hill driving a 275 P2 rear-engined
prototype Ferrari at the Nürburgring in
1965. Above: 1964 275 GTB Ferrari posed against
background of Bay of Naples and Mount Vesuvius.*

speed at 120 or so feels only a little faster.

If you had been driving a $60,000 Boxer Berlinetta, that latest of mid-engined projectiles from Maranello, you'd have been in a car capable of 190 or so that could accelerate from zero to 60 in six seconds. "Who needs such a monster?" you ask. We all do. As we need great symphonies, great sculpture, any great work of art. For the latest car of a mighty line is also an important artistic creation.

And Enzo Ferrari has needed it. For coming in second best in racing or in the construction of superlative cars is something that tough, conniving, mean, arrogant, and sometimes sentimental old Modenese has never borne lightly or easily.

In 1978 Ferrari was very old, about eighty, a king who had succeeded in what he set

365 GT/4 Boxer Berlinetta has a flat twelve-cylinder,
4.4-liter, 360-hp rear engine. Opposed
cylinders give it the name of "Boxer." It can exceed
180 mph. To comply with law, American
bumpers have been added. The engine and other aspects
are at right. The newer 5-liter model hits 190.

out to do some thirty years earlier. There is no greater name than Enzo Ferrari in the world of cars. But he had lost, too. The death of his son Dino, his Crown Prince who died at age twenty-four in 1956, caused him continuing pain. There is no heir to carry on the company. Perhaps this was behind the sale to Fiat in 1969. But Ferrari has remained the absolute monarch of his kingdom, and will remain so until he dies.

Bentley

The Bentley—the *real* Bentley, not those cars Bentleyphiles consider to be Rolls-Royces masquerading as Bentleys— were built for only twelve years. Still, the name Bentley seems to mean as much to some Englishmen as those of Sir Francis Drake, Lord Nelson, and the Beatles combined.

Walter Owen Bentley was born in London in 1888. He had eight brothers and sisters, and they and his parents, plus a squad of servants, inhabited a vast old house near Regents Park. The house succumbed to a German land mine in 1940.

Walter, even more than most Victorian small boys, was crazy about cricket and railways, especially locomotives. After formal schooling at Clifton, which ended at sixteen, he was sent off to serve a five-year premium apprenticeship at the Great Northern Railway shops at Doncaster, for which his parents paid £75. He did however receive wages: five shillings a week. (Henry Royce, too, had learned his craft as a railway apprentice.) In spite of grueling labor, sometimes as a locomotive fireman, he was hooked on railway engines for the rest of his life and cadged rides in their cabs every chance he got.

Bentley's first experience with motor vehicles was with a primitive belt-drive 3-hp Quadrant motorcycle that he bought used in 1906. Soon he was competing in trials and races on various two-wheelers that succeeded the Quadrant. A crude two-cylinder belt-drive Riley, bought while he was still an apprentice, got him started on cars.

When his apprenticeship ended he forsook locomotives as a career and got himself a job with an early taxicab company that had five hundred two-cylinder French Unic cabs on London's streets. He was the assistant to the manager and not only helped oversee maintenance, but tried to prevent the cabbies from diddling the meters to defraud the owners. Cab drivers in 1910 were little different from their present-day descendants.

In 1912 Bentley and his brother Horace raised a few thousand pounds and became the distributors of a French car, the D.F.P. (Doriot, Flandrin et Parent). W. O. Bentley was twenty-four, his brother twenty-seven. The previous D.F.P. distributors had done almost nothing to publicize the cars, but Bentley started tuning them for competition and soon won some minor events. His successes, plus a little advertising and a lot of hard talking to prospective dealers, soon showed in sales of cars.

A few months before World War I, he was in France at the D.F.P. factory talking to Monsieur Doriot about building a sporting version of the car. Bentley noticed an aluminum paperweight in the shape of a piston on Doriot's desk. It gave him the idea that he might try to use aluminum pistons in his cars' engines. He secretly had some cast and machined, and found

Preceding pages: 1929 3-liter Bentley.
The fabric body is by Wylder. The top speed of this
model was about 85 mph. Between 1922 and 1929,
1,629 3-liter models were built, more
than all other models combined. The top speed
of a Red Label was over 85 mph.

that he could squeeze more power out of his engines before piston failure occurred. He kept mum about his aluminum alloy.

Just after this discovery, World War I started, and Bentley found himself an officer in the Royal Naval Air Service. The secret aluminum piston Bentley showed his superiors was soon running up and down inside the cylinders of airplane engines—the 200-hp Rolls-Royce Eagle, the rotary Clerget, and the Sunbeam.

The unreliable Clerget engines of 1915 and 1916 were killing fighter pilots. "Flying the damn things is suicide," one officer said to Bentley, who was spending a lot of his time at aerodromes and in the air over France. So Bentley engaged in combat with the Pooh Bahs of the Admiralty, the Royal Flying Corps, and the Royal Naval Air Service. He raised so much hell that the bureaucrats finally allowed him to go to Coventry, where he and a small staff were to design a better engine. The result was a reliable rotary engine called the B.R.1 (Bentley Rotary 1). British Camels were using them by June, 1917. It was a B.R.1-engined Sopwith Camel flown by Roy Brown that brought down Baron Manfred von Richthofen in 1918. A later 250-hp B.R.2 was in mass production when the war ended.

Bentley was mustered out with a £1,000 gratuity and was told to make a claim to the government for his invention of the B.R.1 and 2. After a fearful hassle he got £8,000. Then the income-tax people tried to snatch part of it back! Bentley won that fight.

During the temporary postwar boom Bentley and his brother made themselves some £20,000 selling D.F.P.'s again, enough to get going on the design of a superquality sporting automobile—the Bentley.

But W. O. had started on the new car even before that boom-time money came in. In January, 1919, he, Harry Varley of the Vauxhall Company, and F. T. Burgess, the former chief designer of Humber cars, had got together to put down on paper what Bentley wanted his new car to be. A company, Bentley Motors Limited, was formed and stock was issued.

It wasn't easy to put together that new Bentley from scratch in postwar England. There were shortages of material, shortages of labor, and every bit had to be made to order by outsiders. For Bentley Motors Ltd. had tiny machine-shop facilities, no foundry, and not much money.

The engine of EX-1 (Experimental No. 1), the first 3-liter Bentley, ran for the first time in October, 1919. Bentley's former sales manager, A. F. C. Hillstead, in his book *Those Bentley Days*, described the occasion: "I had never before witnessed the first starting-up of an entirely new design and, if I felt a thrill, what must W. O.'s feelings have been when something of his own creation was about to come to life? That engine looked very new and proud standing alone on its wooden trestle and, as no exhaust manifold was fitted, I knew we were in for a fairly hefty noise.

"With everything set W. O. pressed the starter switch, the Bendix pinion engaged with the toothed ring on the flywheel, the starter motor came into action, and the psychological moment had arrived. The result was—nothing at all. Not even the vestige of a kick to cheer our hearts. The starter motor did its job valiantly, but out of respect for the hard-working batteries, the switch was released and the ensuing silence could be felt. No one spoke; conversation seemed superfluous, but W. O.'s expression blackened, while Clive Gallop—whose job it was to control the throttle—moved the operating arm in a manner suggesting utter indifference to the whole proceedings. Again the starter switch went home, the motor whirred and the engine rotated as before, but still with no effect. Soon it became obvious that unless something happened fairly soon, the supply of electrical energy would be exhausted. There was an uneasy shuffling of feet, and only a . . . kick on the shin prevented one misguided know-all from offering advice. Then suddenly W. O. spoke. Addressing no one in particular, he said: 'Benzole! Get me some benzole!'

"From that moment the spell was broken. Someone left the room in a hurry and, in a remarkably short time, an orange-coloured can was produced.

"The float-chamber was drained and refilled with the evil smelling spirit; a considerable quantity was added to the main supply tank, and about a pint or so trickled on to the floor. Then once more silence as W. O., as expressionless as ever, pressed the starter switch. Almost at once there was a sharp explosion accompanied by a vivid yellow flash, and—after a moment's hesitation—the air vibrated to a pleasing roar. There was a cheer from the assembled company; W. O. smiled as Gallop gave a wider throttle opening, and then some thoughtful person opened a window. The exhaust note from that engine was strident and, as the room was narrow with both floor and ceiling rickety and resonant, the appalling din is better imagined than described. Some five minutes later a hospital nurse suddenly appeared. She bore a message from the matron of the convalescent home next door, who, so it seemed, had no enthusiasm for the finer points of internal combustion engines. Actually she threatened immediate appeal to the police unless the noise ceased at once. I think we all cursed, but as no one wanted trouble on that memorable occasion, the throttle was opened to its fullest extent and, after one glorious crescendo, the proceedings came to an end. Nevertheless, the first engine of a new breed had made its bow, and 3-liter history was in the melting pot."

The first owner of the first production 3-liter Bentley didn't get his car until September, 1921. He paid a thousand guineas for it—or about $5,250. Over the years there were, of course, many minor changes in the 3-liter Bentley before it went out of production in 1929.

The four-cylinder engine had an 80-mm bore and a long stroke of 149 mm. The long

This 1926 3-liter Bentley is now fitted with a 110-hp, 4½-liter engine. Its original fabric Vanden Plas body was destroyed in an accident, and its present aluminum body is by Cooper of London. The more powerful engine has enabled its owner to reach some 92 mph.

stroke was at least partly due to the British method of horsepower taxation, which was based on cylinder diameter. But a long stroke also gives good torque at low revs. A single overhead camshaft operated four valves per cylinder. The head was not detachable and the camshaft was driven by a vertical shaft at the front of the engine. Two magnetos supplied the sparks to the two spark plugs in each cylinder. A single five-jet Smith carburetor supplied liquid nourishment. These early engines had only a 4.3-to-1 compression ratio, but still pushed out 70 bhp at 3,500 rpm, enough for a speed of 80 mph. The ladder-type frame was high and not too rigid and was suspended on half-elliptic springs. Wheelbase was 130 inches. A Ferodo-lined cone clutch, a four-speed gearbox, and a robust rear axle transmitted the power. All of this sounds rather prosaic, but these specifications were for the Standard model of the early twenties.

Today when we murmur in hushed tones of the great 3-liter Bentley, it is the Red Label Speed model we're talking about. (The

Above: Most 8-liter Bentleys had heavy, luxurious bodywork, quite unlike the sporting body on this 1931 model. Right: Six-cylinder engine of car above developed about 230 hp ; 110 mph was possible. Specially tuned version owned by the late Forrest Lycett was timed at over 141 mph.

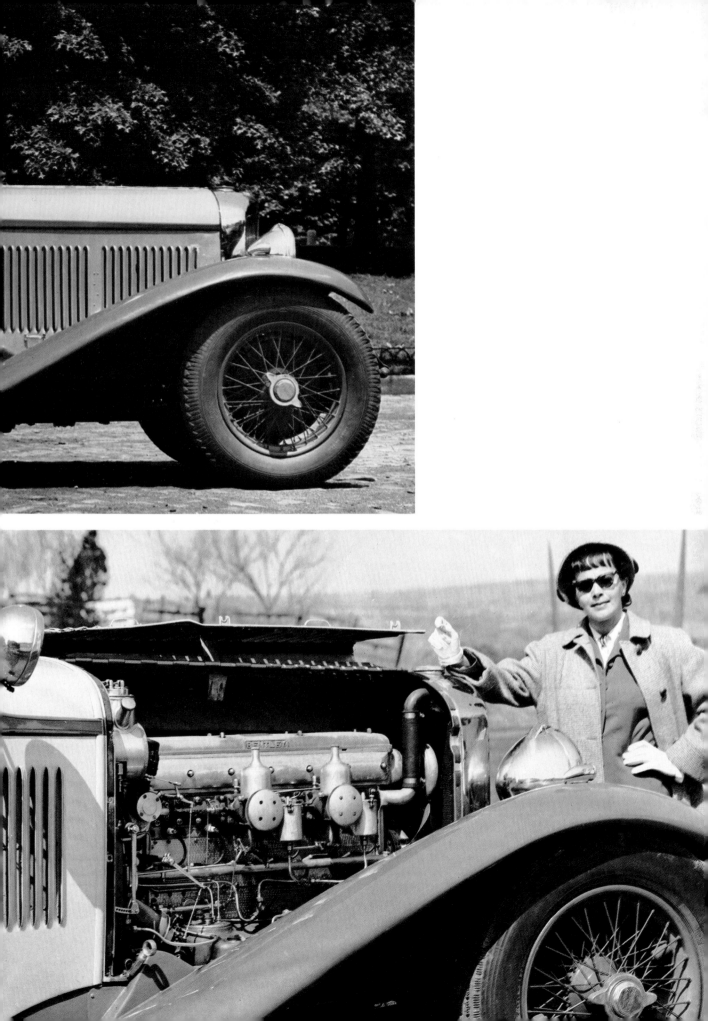

term "Red Label" refers to the color of the background enamel on the radiator badge. Different models usually, but not invariably, bore different colors. Sometimes customers demanded that the enamel match the color of the coachwork.) In 1930 a friend of mine bought a near-new Red Label 3-liter with a fabric Vanden Plas touring body. This one had twin S.U. carburetors and a 5.6-to-1 compression ratio, and developed 85 bhp. Wheelbase was 117½ inches. If we tried hard we could get her up to about 90 mph. And we did try hard. For that old Speed model made us feel impervious to disaster. Compared with the Buicks and Chryslers we'd been used to, the Bentley was a marvel of sure-footedness. Steering was light and direct, braking far better than any we'd known before, and the deep burbling sound from the exhaust pipe made us think that the Bentley's 85 hp must surely be twice that.

There was an even more puissant 3-liter: the Green Label 100-mph model. This one had a shorter chassis—108 inches—and at first only two-seater bodies were fitted. The short chassis was reputed to make it a mite twitchy on wet roads.

Except for some minor competition at Brooklands track, the first big race a Bentley ran in was at Indianapolis in 1922. Someone at Bentley Motors Ltd. must have been out of his mind to enter a sports car against the hot track-racing machines at the Brickyard. Still, the pointed-tail two-seater, whose only modifications were an outside exhaust pipe and higher-compression pistons, didn't actually disgrace itself. It finished thirteenth (some pundits say twentieth) at an average speed of 80 mph. The winner, Jimmy Murphy in a Miller-engined Duesenberg chassis, averaged 94.48 mph.

Three weeks later, three 3-liter Bentleys, one driven by W. O. himself, ran in the Tourist Trophy Race on the Isle of Man. The competition consisted of out-and-out racing machines—Sunbeams, Vauxhalls. The Bentleys had smaller radiators than standard, high-compression pistons, outside exhaust pipes, and pointed tails on their two-seater bodies. It cost only £25 to slightly modify each car thus. All three Bentleys kept going despite rough roads and frightful weather conditions. Only two of the racing cars and all three Bentleys finished. One Bentley, driven by F. C. Clement, came in second behind a Sunbeam. The *Sunday Times* of London said: "Quite the most outstanding feature of the race was the running of the Bentleys." The prestigious *Autocar* agreed: "Surely the Bentley team may claim the greatest credit."

Kudos like these and word of mouth among the cognoscenti soon made the Bentley almost as highly regarded as the Rolls-Royce, a remarkable feat for a car that had been on the market for such a short time.

Still, admired as it was, the Bentley sold poorly. At a thousand guineas it was too expensive. Further, the rich who might have bought it considered it too much of a racing machine. They wanted more luxury for their money. The 3-liter Bentley could perhaps have been sold for less had its castings and forgings

Preceding pages: 4½-liter Bentley (top left) as it appeared in the 1957 British-American rally. Lower left: Cockpit of 3-liter Bentley. Right: Imposing prow of 4½-liter "blower" Bentley. The supercharger lives out front with twin S.U. carburetors; the screen keeps debris out of carburetor intakes.

and gear sets, plus a hundred other bits and pieces, been made in Bentley's own workshops. But the company was ridiculously undercapitalized. There was never enough money to build a proper factory. Until the very end, in 1931, Bentley Ltd. lived hand-to-mouth.

It was their remarkable series of victories at Le Mans—*les vingt-quatre Heures du Mans*—that elevated the Bentleys into big green chariots of the gods in the minds of worshipful Englishmen. It also elevated the Le Mans race into prominence, mostly because the Bentley-loving English thought that any race that Bentleys won just *had* to be important.

It wasn't W. O. Bentley's idea to race a 3-liter Bentley at that obscure twenty-four-hour race near the small provincial French town of Le Mans. It was Captain John Duff's. He was a Bentley customer who had broken the Double Twelve Hours record at Brooklands track in 1922 in his own 3-liter. He'd met Bentley's sales manager, A. F. C. Hillstead, in the street and said: "You might tell W. O. that if he'll prepare the car and lend me a mechanic, I'll buy a new Speed model and enter it at Le Mans. Ring me up this afternoon."

That's how the Bentley's great years at Le Mans began.

With F. C. Clement, head of Bentley's experimental department (he seems to have been the whole department), as codriver, the Duff 3-liter set off on its twenty-four-hour run in the 1923 Le Mans race. The road at Le Mans wasn't paved in those days and during the night a flying stone broke one of the Bentley's headlights. This caused a bit of a slowdown. With daylight Duff was able to put his foot down and break the lap record at 64.7 mph. Then came disaster. A stone went through the gas tank and it took a couple of hours to patch the hole with cork and soap. (I wish I knew how they managed that.) In spite of Clement breaking the lap record again (the first sports-car lap record at Le Mans), the Bentley couldn't manage better than fourth place.

In 1924 the Duff 3-liter, again with Clement as codriver, and now with four-wheel brakes (which made for faster cornering), won the race. This time they'd been smart enough to put wire-mesh stone guards on the headlights and under the gas tank. In the next year's race the two Bentleys the factory entered would have done better if they'd remained locked up at home in England. One ran out of gas, the other caught fire when a carburetor float chamber fell off. The 1925 race is notable because it was the first time drivers had to sprint to their cars in the now-famous "Le Mans start." At that time, too, the drivers not only had to vault into their cars and then start them, they also had to erect the tops.

No cigar in 1926, either.

The story of the Bentley's exploits at Le Mans in 1927 has been done to death, but I daren't ignore it here.

After the contretemps of 1925 and 1926 the Bentley factory had its blood up for a win, by God. Three cars were entered by the

factory: the 3-liter "Old No. 7" (so called because it had borne that number in 1926) driven by its owner, Dr. J. D. Benjafield, and my friend S. C. H. "Sammy" Davis; another 3-liter driven by the Baron d'Erlanger and George Duller; and a prototype of a new 4½-liter car with F. C. Clement and L. Callingham aboard.

For a time everything went well. On only his second lap Clement broke the lap record at 72 mph, then broke it again and again. At about 9:30 P.M., as it began to get dark, things started to come apart.

Callingham, leaving White House corner in the 4½ at some 90 mph, found that a Frenchman in a Th. Schneider had got himself into a spin and was half blocking the road. Callingham took frantic avoiding action, but hit the Schneider hard, then rolled over partly into a ditch on the opposite side, blocking the other half of the road. A small French car managed to zigzag through, but Duller in his 3-liter missed the Schneider and hit the Bentley squarely in the stern. Duller, a steeplechase jockey, purposely caromed out of his seat at the instant of impact. Dr. Benjafield, recounting the story later, said: "Describing a graceful parabola, turning numerous somersaults . . . Duller cleared the hedge and landed in a nice soft field." He then rushed down the road to stop Sammy Davis from piling Old No. 7 into the rapidly expanding Bentley junkyard. He was too late. As Davis later described it, in his book *A Racing Motorist:* "As I swung round that right-hand turn, on the road in front was a scatter of

*Above: Bentley advertisement on the cover of
the prestigious British magazine,* The Motor.
*Opposite: Engine of 4 1/2-liter supercharged Bentley.
Carburetors which seem to be missing
are outdoors, in front of the radiator, where
they are attached to the blower.*

earth, a piece or so of splintered wood; the thing flashed an immediate warning, for I had seen such traces before in the 1924 Grand Prix, when, round the corner, another car had crashed.

"Even then it did not occur to me to do more than slow a little and be ready. The car swung round White House corner almost at full speed. I jammed down the brake pedal, tried to spin the wheel, and skidded broadside on, for, white and horrible in the headlights' beam, an appalling tangle of smashed cars appeared right across the road in front! With the rending crash of riven metal we slid right into the mass and brought up all standing with a shock that threw me hard against the wheel. All the lights went out."

Old No. 7 was a wreck. It had a broken wheel and its front axle was bent and pushed backward. Only one headlight worked, and that pointed in the wrong direction. A running board and fender were in tatters. The frame was bent. Davis backed out of the shambles. At the Bentley pit, W. O., who had resigned himself to losing all three machines *and* the race, tried to talk Davis out of continuing.

Said Davis, "I am going on." He tied up the battery, which was dangling from the running board, and did minor surgery elsewhere with spit and string.

Davis knew it was hopeless to try to win, but with practically no brakes, odd steering, and one cockeyed headlight he pushed on for 214 miles before Benjafield took over. It

146

started to rain; Benjafield had to stop now and then to tie up the battery. He replaced a side light with a police lantern.

At dawn only a French Ariès was still ahead. W. O. had the gall to give Benjafield the "faster" signal. He had noticed that the Ariès' engine sounded unwell and decided that making it go faster to keep it ahead of the Bentley might do it in.

W. O. was right. The Ariès soon stopped with a very sick engine. Old No. 7 won as the British love to win, by almost losing.

That 4½-liter Bentley that poor Callingham had demolished was the precursor of a new model, an enlarged version of the 3-liter. Before the 4½-liter car appeared, however, a bigger six-cylinder, 6½-liter Bentley made its debut in 1926. This was the Big Six, which some pundits claim was so much like the H6B Hispano-Suiza that it couldn't have been mere coincidence. In fact, it had exactly the same bore and stroke as the Hispano engine—100 x 140 mm.

The Big Six was born in a rather odd

Top left: 4 ¹/₂-liter Bentley engine.
Bottom: Bentley boys at Le Mans, 1929: D'Erlanger,
Barnato, Birkin, Jack Dunfee, Kidston,
Benjafield, Chassagne, and Clement. Above:
Bernard Rubin empties gas cans into boxlike funnel
during 1929 pit stop at Le Mans.

Frontal aspect of a recently restored
8-liter Bentley. Many big Bentleys that originally
carried ponderous, closed coachwork
have been rebuilt with sumptuous,
open bodies. I do not believe, however,
that this car was ever a limousine.

way. The 3-liter, it was felt, just shouldn't have luxury coachwork imposed on its light, sporting, and overly flexible frame, and it was hoped that a new model capable of being fitted with closed bodies might bring in some much-needed cash. An experimental 4¼-liter six-cylinder car with a longer, heavier frame was, therefore, constructed. To test it in 1924 W. O. had it fitted with a remarkably ugly Freestone and Webb body, stuffed it full of passengers, and took it over to France to watch the French Grand Prix. To disguise the car it was fitted with an atrocious-looking hexagonal radiator shell and registered as "The Sun."

To compound his problems, Bentley was also trying out the then-new Dunlop balloon tires, which required only 16 pounds of air. They were wonderfully comfortable, but kept blowing out under the 2½-ton weight of the heavily laden "Sun."

As he was cruising along at some 65 mph and worrying about blowouts, Bentley caught sight of another peculiar car trailing a dust cloud and converging from a side road toward the same Y junction he himself was approaching. Both cars sped up and got into the Y simultaneously. Bentley and the people in the other machine immediately saw through the disguises. The other camouflaged car was one of the new Phantom I Rolls-Royces on test. Naturally, both drivers, their blood up, just had to race. And side by side they roared down the dusty poplar-lined *Route nationale* for kilometer after kilometer. Evenly matched, neither car

could have bested the other had they continued all the way to the English Channel. The race ended when the cap of one of the Rolls-Royce's people blew off and the car was stopped so that he might retrieve it.

Back in England, W. O. and his associates, certain that Rolls-Royce would increase their new car's power, decided that they'd better increase their machine's power, too, The 6½-liter engine was the answer.

The 6½-liter engine, like the 3-liter, had four valves per cylinder and a single overhead camshaft. But in the interest of silence, since the car was to be not only a high-speed tourer but also a dignified town carriage, the drive to the camshaft would not be via a geared vertical shaft. Bentley devised a system of three long coupling rods driven at the crankshaft end by a miniature three-throw crankshaft and connected to another miniature crankshaft attached to the camshaft. With a single carburetor and a 4.4-to-1 compression ratio, the Big Six's 6½-liter engine developed 140 bhp. About 85 mph was achievable.

But there was another, far more exciting, 6½-liter Bentley. This was the Speed Six of 1929, which had high-compression pistons— 5.3 to 1 (not much by today's standards)—twin S.U. carburetors, and a higher-lift camshaft. By 1930 180 bhp was developed. In racing, Speed Sixes could quite easily exceed 100 mph. Although a large and heavy car—wheelbase for the short-chassis model was 140½ inches and weight with an open body was about 4,800 pounds—it was so nicely balanced and so easily and accurately steered that it felt like a much smaller sports car on the road. A 6½-liter Bentley chassis cost about £1,500.

Money was still a terrible problem at Bentley Motors Ltd. It had cost much more than the limited finances of the company could bear to get the 6½-liter car through its experimental stages and into production. Things looked black. But a millionaire international playboy, gambler, speedboat racer, boxer, racing driver ("the best driver we ever had," said W. O. Bentley), and shrewd financier, Woolf Barnato, bailed the company out in 1926.

"Babe" Barnato was the son of Barnett Isaacs, who had gone to Africa almost penniless at twenty-one, somehow got into diamond mining, amassed a huge amount of money, and changed his name to Barney Barnato. Through a deal with Cecil Rhodes, Barnato and his family acquired a near-monopoly on the mining of diamonds and gold in some sections of southern Africa. During a trip to England with Woolf, who was then an infant, Barney Barnato disappeared overboard. A complex series of lawsuits involving Woolf resulted. Woolf ended up with millions of pounds, and like the adventurous and very rich young man he was, he naturally owned and raced Bentley motorcars. And with considerable success.

Babe Barnato was as sharp a businessman as his father had been. His terms for financing Bentley Motors were very tough, indeed. For example, all of the original one-pound shares in the company were to be revalued to one shilling per share, which, of course, wiped out some of the early stockholders.

What was perhaps the most desirable of all the Bentleys, the four-cylinder 4½-liter model, appeared in 1927. It came out after the Big Six was announced but before the Speed Six was developed. It was, in fact, a 3-liter with a bigger engine. And since it had the same 100 x 140-mm cylinder dimensions as the 6½-liter models, many parts were interchangeable. Open-bodied 4½'s developed 110 bhp at 3,500 rpm. In Le Mans trim the 4½-liter cars' horsepower went up to 130. The standard 4½'s were capable of 92 mph; the Le Mans cars were about 5 mph faster.

The fastest 4½-liter Bentleys were the fifty or so blown models. W. O. hated the idea of supercharging his engines. He said it was "against all my engineering principles." But Sir Henry "Tim" Birkin, one of the top Bentley drivers, persuaded famous designer Amherst Villiers to design one for his 4½, and then charmed Barnato into going along with the idea. The money for the first supercharged 4½'s came from the very rich, the Hon. Dorothy Paget. When Tim Birkin talked Barnato into allowing him to enter a team of "Blower" Bentleys in the 1930 Le Mans race, the Bentley company was required under the regulations to build fifty of them to be sold as catalog models.

The Bentley blowers, which, with their carburetors, stuck out forward of the radiators, provided a 10-pound boost on standard models and a 12-pound boost on the Le Mans cars, which then developed 240 bhp at 4,200 rpm. Sadly, no Blower Bentley ever won a race, and W. O. put part of the blame for the demise of the Bentley company on the fifty overly expensive supercharged machines.

In 1928, three 4½-liter Bentleys were entered at Le Mans. For the first time it was not required that tops be raised. There was strong competition that year from four Chryslers and a Stutz Black Hawk. The Stutz, driven by Frenchmen Brisson and Bloch, came close to winning when the radiator on the Woolf Barnato-Bernard Rubin Bentley came adrift and lost much of its water. But the Stutz had its troubles, too. Its top gear kept jumping out of mesh. In the end the Bentley won by 8 miles.

A Speed Six first ran at Le Mans in 1929. Driven by Woolf Barnato and Sir Henry Birkin, it set the year's lap record at 82.984 mph at the ninety-ninth lap. There was an American challenge from three Stutzes, a du Pont, and two Chryslers. The four other Bentleys were 4½'s. Just before the race ended the four Bentleys still running were in the lead. But they were overdue. Had they all broken down? Not at all. They had pulled up at the side of the road, so they might finish in line-ahead formation like so many battleships in a naval review. With the Barnato-Birkin first, the Bentleys took the first four places. It was their finest hour.

Although two Speed Sixes won again in 1930, there wasn't quite the drama of the previous year's race, despite the presence of two blown 4½-liter Bentleys entered by the Hon. Dorothy Paget, and of Rudolf Caracciola in a supercharged Mercedes-Benz. The Mercedes, after a brilliant run, was at last put out by Barnato's and Birkin's harrying tactics, which forced Caracciola to overuse his supercharger with deleterious effects on his engine.

In addition to many successes in other competitions, the Bentleys had won four times at Le Mans: 1927–1930. Only Alfa Romeo ever equaled that record (1931–1934).

If you were a Hollywood movie star, an Indian maharajah, a young duke, *the* car to own in those feverish years between World War I and the Great Depression was a Bentley. But these elegant types, although Bentley lovers, were not of the inner circle of Bentleyphiles— the legendary "Bentley Boys"—purportedly rich, champagne-drinking habitués of gambling clubs, luxurious West End flats, and yachts, complete with mistresses, at Monte Carlo. This gaudy picture was certainly true of many, if not most, of the Bentley Boys. But they were also the men who drove the Bentleys to victory. Their leader was, of course, Babe Barnato. And then there were the wealthy Australian Bernard Rubin and the indomitable Sammy Davis, who talked to me about Bentleys only a few years ago, when he was in his late eighties. The furiously fast J. D. Benjafield, M.D., of Harley Street and Le Mans; Baron d'Erlanger, the international banker-playboy; Frank Clement, Bentley's only professional driver, who drove Bentleys in more races than any other Bentley

Boy; Sir Henry Birkin; and about a dozen others make up the short list.

In his autobiography, W. O. Bentley reminisces that he once drove an 8-liter Bentley from Dieppe to Cannes in one day without having to switch on the headlights. He cruised at about 85 mph for hours on end. Imagine such performance almost fifty years ago on the roads of those days!

The 8-liter Bentley that arrived in 1930 was not meant to be a sporting machine. It was a luxury car in the class of the Rolls-Royce, the Hispano-Suiza, or the Isotta Fraschini. But it was still undeniably a Bentley with Bentley bloodlines, and some owners, eschewing the vast closed coachwork the 8-liter was designed to carry, insisted that their cars be fitted with open sporting bodies. These lighter bodies were installed on the shorter of the two chassis offered, the one with a 144-inch wheelbase. The standard chassis had a 156-inch wheelbase. A friend of mine owned one, and at times I drove the formidable machine, which was fitted with a light close-coupled touring body. It handled with surprising ease. The steering was light, but its turning circle would seem small only to the captain of a supertanker. The 8-liter's six-cylinder engine was exactly like that in the 6½-liter model, but with 110 x 140-mm cylinders, which added up to 7,983 cc. Horsepower was 225.

Several times I saw 100 mph on the speedometer of the 8-liter, and my friend who owned the car said that he'd often reached 110.

Specially lightened and tuned examples, like that owned by the late Forrest Lycett, were very much quicker. In 1956 Lycett's car was timed at 141.7 mph for the flying kilometer. Only one hundred 8-liters were ever built. Cars costing £3,000 didn't sell too well in 1930 and 1931.

As a last-ditch effort to stave off disaster the Bentley company's directors decided to build a 4-liter car with a pushrod engine and using the big, heavy 8-liter frame. It was not a success and did not prevent the inevitable collapse. A receiver was appointed.

D. Napier and Son, builders of the great Napier cars of Edwardian days and of a not-too-successful ohc six in the early 1920's and, more recently, important builders of airplane engines, became interested in taking over the Bentley company. A new car, a 6¼-liter Napier-Bentley, was designed. But it was not to be. In court at the receiver's sale, which was expected to be a cut-and-dried approval of Napier's bid for the company, another bidder arose and offered a price only some hundreds of pounds higher. The surprise bidder was the British Central Equitable Trust. Some days later, W. O. found out what B.C.E.T. really was. It was Rolls-Royce.

If late some night you happen to be near the southeast corner of Grosvener Square in London, and you hear a deep and gentle burbling as from Bentley exhausts, you're hearing ghosts. For it was there, near where Birkin and Barnato and Rubin lived, that the Bentley Boys left their big green cars while partying.

4 ½-liter "blower" Bentley.
Fifty of these cars were built to qualify
Bentley for the Le Mans race that year.
Tremendous cost was partly responsible for the
company's demise. Despite 240 hp and high speed,
no supercharged 4 ½ ever won a race.

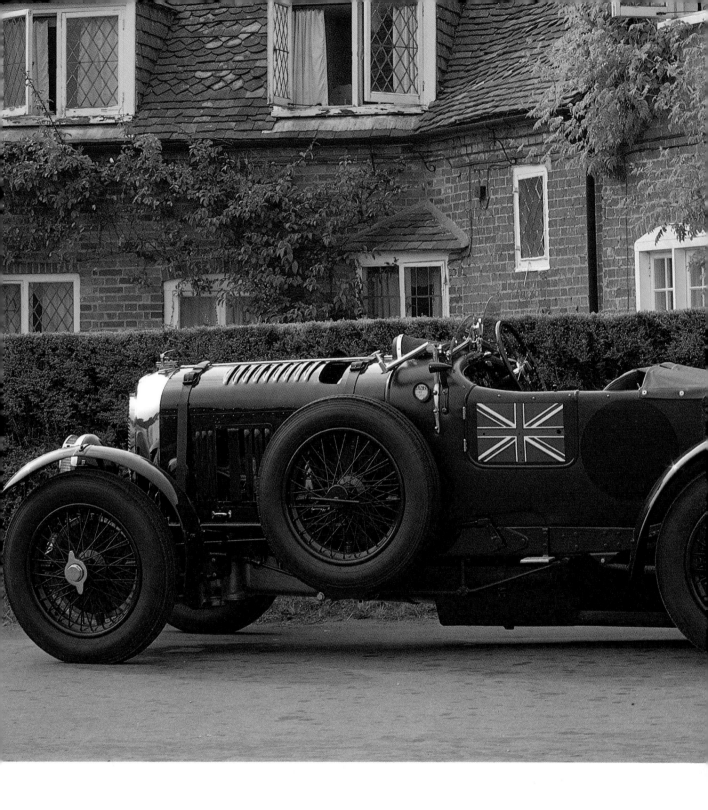

Hispano-Suiza

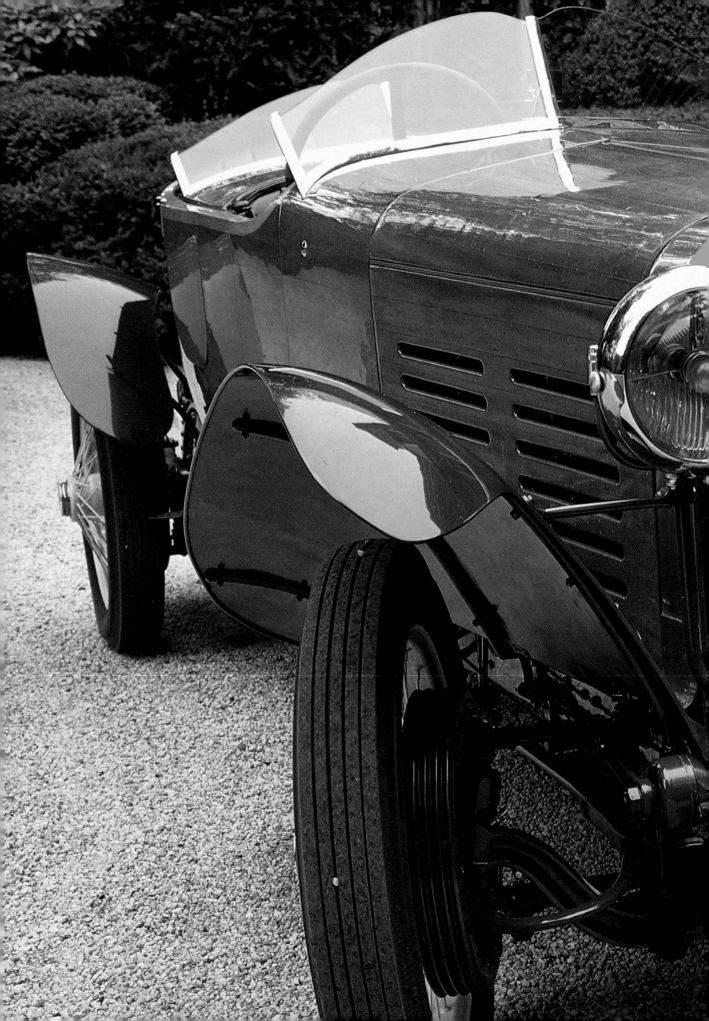

The Hispano-Suiza was in its day the unchallengeable king of motorcars. Neither the Rolls-Royce, nor the Isotta Fraschini, nor even that most regal of Bugattis, the Golden Bug, surpassed it in design, in craftsmanship, or in the manner of its going.

And the Hispano-Suiza most deserving of the royal accolade was, in this writer's view, the incomparable H6, known in France as the 32CV and in Britain as the 37.2 hp. It was the kind of car that, suitably dressed in stuffy formal coachwork, might be used by a stiffnecked superrich captain of finance to transport his jewel-encrusted females to the opening of the Paris opera. Or if its owner was the kind of gilded blood who in the 1920's wished to convey at high speed to the Côte d'Azur more young ladies from the Folies-Bergère than could be accommodated within the narrow confines of a Type 43 Bugatti, he could get them there aboard a Hispano fitted with a yachtlike, open, wooddecked, double-cowled touring body. Or, if he was so minded, his car could be denuded of fenders and lights, then driven the length of Italy's boot and across the straits to Sicily, where he might give the Targa Florio a go. The H6 Hispano-Suiza was hardly a small racing machine, but André Dubonnet, whose name still graces the bottles of an apéritif wine, did just that and once managed a creditable sixth place against a gaggle of Alfa Romeos and Bugattis.

The H6 Hispano-Suiza created a sensation when it made its first appearance at the Paris Salon in 1919. And well it might have. For even after sixty years an examination of a surviving Hispano (and there are many survivors) still inspires awe. The H6 Hispano-Suiza's six-cylinder, 6½-liter (100-mm bore x 140-mm stroke) engine was based largely on the firm's V-8 airplane engines, which had so successfully powered the French Spads, the British SE-5's, and other Allied flying machines of World War I. During the war twenty-one factories had produced over 50,000 of them. In France, famous car manufacturers Peugeot, Brasier, and Ariès were some of the contractors building parts. In England, Wolseley built it as the Wolseley Viper, and in the United States it was built in the old Crane-Simplex factory in New Jersey and by Wright-Martin in Long Island City. At the peak of production, ninety Hispano-Suiza engines built by 35,000 workers were delivered every day. Flying aces René Fonck, Eddie Rickenbacker, and Georges Guynemer had been among the many Allied fighter pilots who depended on the Hispano engine, which not only weighed a third less than the Germans' Mercedes engine, but had some five hundred fewer parts. It was from the stork insignia that emblazoned the fuselages of the machines in Guynemer's squadron that the "Flying Stork" radiator ornament of postwar Hispano-Suizas was derived.

The valves of the 6½-liter H6 engine were, like those of the aero engine, operated by

*Preceding pages: The 1923 H6B Hispano-Suiza
had a six-cylinder, 6 ¹/₂-liter, 135-hp overhead-camshaft
engine and was capable of some 90 mph. The
Paris-built body of this splendid machine is exquisitely
planked in tulipwood attached to boatlike ribs by
thousands of gleaming copper fastenings.*

a single overhead camshaft that was driven by a vertical shaft at the front of the engine. The nitrided steel cylinders were threaded and screwed into the aluminum alloy block, which the instruction book refers to as a "cooling jacket . . . made corrosion-proof by a special process of enameling under pressure." The seven-bearing crankshaft was a most expensive polished steel jewel with completely circular webs. Made from a 700-pound solid billet of steel, it weighed only 90 pounds after it had been machined. I remember seeing one hanging from a rafter in Zumbach's New York shop during some mysterious operation on a Hispano engine. When a mechanic struck it lightly with a rod, it rang like a tuning fork.

Ignition was by twin Delco distributors and coils to twelve spark plugs—two per cylinder. The dual carburetor had, according to the instruction book, "a double rotary slide valve" instead of the usual butterfly. The float chamber was instantly detachable by means of a lever. The huge oil-filling orifice under a hinged cover could take a modern can of oil at one gulp (although oil in cans was unknown in the twenties).

The H6 engine delivered 135 bhp at a mere 3,500 rpm. But at only 2,000 rpm it still delivered 120 bhp. Compression was only 4½ to 1. Tremendous torque was developed. With a high axle ratio of 3.37 to 1, it was easy to crawl along at 4 mph in top gear.

Early H6's transmitted power to a three-speed gearbox through a cone clutch, but later models used a plate clutch. The drive shaft was unusual in being in two sections. The forward half was open, the after half enclosed in a torque tube.

The chassis was a simple ladder type suspended on half-elliptic springs. Very early chassis had no shock absorbers at all. Later, various types were installed: friction Hartfords, Houdailles, and finally even those wildly complex self-adjusting De Rams beloved of Ettore Bugatti.

An unusual feature of the H6 was its firewall. Built of sheet aluminum and asbestos, it was airtight. All controls including the steering column, which passed through it, were so accurately fitted that little engine heat reached the car's occupants.

The H6's four-wheel braking system was surprisingly advanced for 1919. Rolls-Royce, for example, still had braking on only its rear wheels. When Rolls at last went to braking on all wheels in 1924, Hispano's servomechanism, which applied the brakes via a gear-driven clutch on the side of the gearbox, was, with some modification, incorporated. Rolls-Royce paid Hispano-Suiza a licensing fee.

The H6, 37.2-hp Hispano-Suiza was capable of some 90 mph—very fast indeed in 1919.

But there were more muscular variations of the H6. In 1922 at the Autumn Grand Prix at Monza in Italy, a Hispano-Suiza driven by André Dubonnet took first place. It had a slightly larger engine—6.9 liters (with a 102-mm

bore instead of 100 mm)—and higher compression (still only 5.75 to 1) and put out some 150 bhp. With light bodywork on a shorter, slightly lower chassis and the high rear-axle ratio at 2.8 to 1, 110 mph was possible. This special model was called the Monza. Only a half-dozen or so were ever built.

In 1923 five Hispano factory racing-team cars had their engines' bores increased to 110 mm instead of the H6's normal 100 mm. This raised their capacity to 8 liters. After they won a race at Boulogne in France they were dubbed Boulogne models. Their British R.A.C. horsepower rating was 45 hp. The factory did not, it seems, call production 8-liter cars, which were first marketed in 1924, Boulogne models, but H6C's. But the name has nevertheless stuck. Today there is some confusion. Purists insist that only the five racing models were Boulognes. To add to the confusion, in 1923 the factory started calling the 6½-liter H6 model the H6B.

The 45-hp H6C was a very quick machine. With a light touring body it was possible to approach 100 mph. It was one of these Boulognes that took part in the famous twenty-four-hour match race with a Stutz Black Hawk in 1928 at Indianapolis.

The race came about in a most peculiar way. At the 1927 motor show at Olympia in London, C. F. Kettering of General Motors had been loudly claiming that a Cadillac was superior to a Rolls-Royce. At a dinner the following evening his boast was discussed by some outraged Britons who didn't think *any* American car could be better than "the Best Car in the World." F. E. Moskovics, president of Stutz and the only American at the dinner, leaped to the defense of American automobiles and suggested that one of his Stutzes be pitted against a Rolls. No one, it seems, took up that challenge. But G. T. Weymann, the builder of the famous flexible fabric bodies that bore his name, spoke up.

"I'll race if you let me run my Hispano against your Stutz."

"Done," said Moskovics.

The next day Kettering saw Moskovics and said, "I understand that to prove a Cadillac can beat a Rolls-Royce from Detroit to Dayton, you bet $25,000 that a Stutz can beat a Hispano-Suiza in a twenty-four-hour race at Indianapolis."

The 8-liter Hispano shot ahead of the 5-liter Stutz straight eight from the start. The driver of the Stutz, not realizing that he had twenty-four hours in which to catch the Hispano, overrevved in the gears and damaged the valve gear. After that the sick Stutz hadn't a chance. Nineteen hours and twenty minutes later the Hispano-Suiza had covered 1,357.5 miles, the Stutz only 732.5. Moskovics conceded the race and paid Weymann.

Moskovics asked that the race be continued with a fresh Stutz, this time without prize money. Weymann was willing. And the Hispano, perhaps a bit out of tune from its run, started against the healthy new Stutz. Twenty hours and thirty minutes had gone by since the

Top left: Alfonso Hispano, performing in contemporary British vintage-car race, survives from days of dashing advertisement at right. Bottom left: Beautiful Grebel headlight of car on pages 156–157. Right: Magnificent H6B engine.

161

first start, and only three and a half hours of the twenty-four remained. This time the Stutz came out 7.5 miles ahead. Weymann then bought a Stutz and entered it in the 1928 twenty-four-hour Le Mans race. There the Stutz almost beat the Bentleys.

It should be pointed out that in 1928 a Stutz Black Hawk speedster cost only $4,895 in the United States. The cheapest H6B Hispano-Suiza then cost circa $20,000 in New York.

It was in the thirties that I saw André Dubonnet in Zumbach's in New York with a most remarkable 8-liter H6C Hispano-Suiza chassis. This Hispano had a rather complex independent front suspension and M. Dubonnet had stopped off at Zumbach's for some adjustments to his chassis, with which he was bound for General Motors in Detroit. I've heard that he also had with him large quantities of his apéritif wine and other liquid comestibles for the entertainment of G.M. executives.

We next saw Dubonnet's suspension on Chevrolets, of all things.

It was during the early 1930's, too, that I drove a Kellner-bodied Boulogne roadster for the first and only time. The famous Ray Gilhooley, who was then engaged in selling used foreign cars and who earlier had given the name "a Gilhooley" to the kind of spin he performed when he'd had an accident in an Isotta Fraschini in the 1914 Indianapolis 500, was trying to sell the lovely Hispano to me. It was the same car that was later owned by the noted Hispanophile

Alex Ulmann; it now resides at Briggs Cunningham's Museum in Costa Mesa, California.

I still remember how amazed I was at the handling, the quick steering, and the remarkably efficient braking of that big car. Used to Model A Fords and such, I was awed by its power and drove it in too timid a fashion to suit Gilhooley, who demanded that I relinquish the wheel to him. He then drove the big Hispano as if it were a Bugatti half its size. Downshifting (which was hardly necessary), cutting in and out of traffic, terrifying taxi drivers (and me, too), he gave a virtuoso performance. I did not, however, buy the Hispano from him. I thought $150 plus my Model A Ford was too expensive for a five-year-old used car.

The Hispano-Suizas were the creations of a great Swiss engineer, Mark Birkigt. At first the cars were built only in Barcelona—hence the "Spanish-Swiss" name. Birkigt's background was not unlike that of Henry Royce. Both had in their youth been involved with railroads, Royce with steam and Birkigt with electric locomotives in Switzerland. During World War I both men built aero engines.

Birkigt, born in Geneva in 1878, was only twenty years old when he arrived in Spain to help design electric locomotives. This led to his involvement in 1899 with a Captain La Cuadra, who was trying to build electric-powered buses. By 1900 he and the Captain had formed a company to build the La Cuadra motorcar. This ambitious enterprise soon failed. The company was then taken over by a Señor

162

Castro, who renamed it with the resounding title of J. Castro Fabrica Hispano-Suiza de Automoviles. Three years later this outfit petered out, too. In June, 1904, it became the Sociedad Hispano-Suiza Fabrica de Automoviles, which for almost forty years would build some of the greatest motorcars of all time.

During the next decade Birkigt turned out some brilliantly innovative designs, including even a supercharged engine as early as 1912. In 1911 he had designed a four-cylinder twin-overhead-camshaft engine with hemispherical combustion chambers not unlike those in the famous racing Peugeots. But Birkigt, not Peugeot, had, it seems, been first with the twin-cam head. The design had been pirated by Hispano's race driver Paul Zucarelli and designer Ernest Henry, who had worked for Hispano but had recently joined Peugeot. A legal hassle resulted and Hispano-Suiza emerged the victor.

But Birkigt was sure he had an even better design for a single-ohc *voiturette* racing engine he was building. This incorporated a supercharger consisting of a two-cylinder reciprocating pump that not only pumped mixture into the cylinders but also sucked the burnt gases out through an extra exhaust valve. During tests cracks appeared in the blower's cylinders, and the cars were not raced.

There had, of course, been at least one earlier use of supercharging in racing cars. The American Chadwick, which ran in the 1908 Vanderbilt Cup Race, had had a blower not too different from Birkigt's.

Hispano-Suiza had started racing in 1909, at first without great success. But in 1910, in *voiturette* races for cars smaller and lighter than the big brutes engaged in Grand Prix racing, Birkigt's Hispanos showed what they could do. The usual single- and twin-cylinder machines engaged in *voiturette* contests were, due to capacity regulations in which only the bore was limited, most peculiar devices indeed. The 1910 Lion-Peugeot, for example, had an engine with an 80-mm bore and the fantastically long stroke of 260 mm. Its hood was so tall that the driver could not see over it. He had to peer along its side. In the 1910 Coupe de l'Auto at Boulogne in France, Birkigt entered rather more normal machines with four-cylinder T-head engines, though they still had the long stroke of 200 mm. Driven by Zucarelli, a Hispano-Suiza took first place. It was the first time a four-cylinder car won the race.

The story goes that Alfonso XIII, the king of Spain, who had long been a Hispano-Suiza enthusiast, became excited by the victory and wanted a similar car for his own use on his own highways.

The result in 1912 was the Alfonso XIII, the T-15, one of the first great sports cars. It had a four-cylinder, 3,620-cc (80 x 180-mm) T-head engine, a multidisc clutch (later models had cone clutches), and three-speed transmissions (four speeds after 1913). Springs were half-elliptic. The specifications sound rather dull, but the Alfonsos were far from dull. They were fast for 1912—75 mph or better. Their steering

was delightfully light and accurate, and they had a fine sporting look. In fact, they were in their own way a sort of Spanish version of that most wonderful early American sports car, the T-head Mercer Raceabout, whose specifications weren't all that different from the Alfonso's.

But the Alfonso was not entirely Spanish for very long. At about the time of its introduction Hispano-Suiza moved some of its operations to Paris, first at an old trolley-car barn in Levallois-Perret, where most of the Alfonsos were built. Later Hispanos were built at Bois-Colombes, near Paris. Some Alfonsos were built in the Barcelona factory until 1920.

Above and bottom right: Sporting 1924
H6C Boulogne model had a bigger engine than
H6B—8 liters instead of 6 1/2. Top right:
1912 Alfonso T-15 Hispano was a
favorite mount of World War I fighter
pilots. Its top speed was 75 mph.

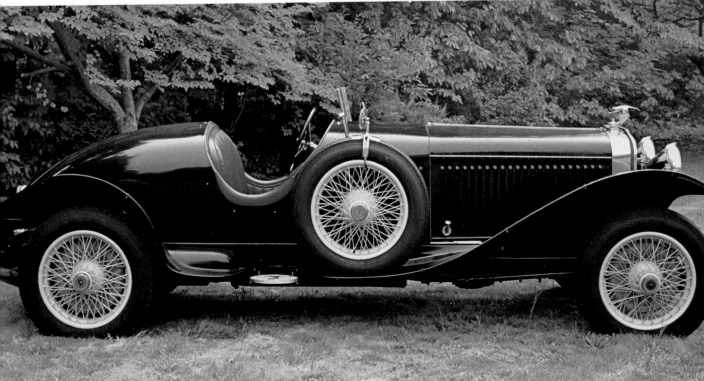

Recently I was going through some faded photographs of World War I fighter pilots. A surprising number of these youths were leaning on or sitting in Alfonsos.

In 1931 the various versions of the superb H6 gave way to Mark Birkigt's super-luxury car, his Tipo 68 V-12, known also as the J-12. The first Tipo 68's had a 9,424-cc engine. The later Tipo 68 Bis had its capacity increased to 11,310 cc. Although one wonders why such an increase was considered necessary, since the smaller engine, which was rated at 220 hp at 3,000 rpm, put out rather more than its rating. The 68 Bis engine was also too conservatively rated at 250 hp. The engines were built in Mark Birkigt's usual superlative style. Like those in the H6's, the twelve steel cylinders were screwed into aluminum blocks that formed "cooling jackets." But the design of the engine differed from that in the H6 in no longer having an overhead camshaft. The V-12 engine used pushrods and rockers to work the valves. Birkigt almost certainly took what seems a retrograde step in the interest of silence, since it must be admitted that the valve gear of an H6 clattered more than just a bit. After all, valve clearance was considerable—eighty-thousandths of an inch. The V-12, on the other hand, ran with incomparably hushed smoothness despite being a tiger on the road.

A V-12 Hispano-Suiza weighing over 5,000 pounds would accelerate from zero to 60 mph in twelve seconds! Fantastic for a big seven-passenger luxury machine in 1932. Top

Top: Most Hispano-Suizas of the 1920's were fitted with heavy formal bodywork but still had fine performance. Bottom: V-12, 11.3-liter Type 68 Bis with two-seater coupe coachwork by Saoutchik. The V-12, which first appeared in 1931, was capable of more than 110 mph.

speed was some 110 mph. Some owners said their cars were even faster.

The chassis, which came in different wheelbase lengths—135, 146, 150, and a lordly 156 inches—could carry almost any kind of coachwork a *carrossier* might dream up. And V-12 Hispano-Suiza bodywork by such great French body builders as Kellner, Binder, Saoutchik, and Figoni et Falaschi has never been surpassed. Hispano-Suiza did not stoop to building coachwork.

The chassis of V-12 Hispanos were deceptively simple, if very tough, ladder types mounted on half-elliptic springs all around. Roadholding and the 2½-turn lock-to-lock steering were remarkably good, but it was the braking of the big heavy cars that most impressed testers writing for the British *Autocar* almost fifty years ago. For a Hispano they tried stopped in 26 feet from 30 mph. In those days it was considered almost physically impossible for any car to stop from 30 mph in less than 30 feet. Hispano, of course, still used the gearbox-actuated brake-servo that Mark Birkigt had pioneered on the H6's.

The gearbox of the V-12 had only three speeds. Top gear was usually a high 2.72 to 1, but lower ratios were obtainable if a customer wanted to carry coachwork of Pullman-car proportions. Synchromesh was fitted.

Hispano-Suiza V-12's were not as expensive as you might think—only some $18,000 with top-quality coachwork. But there was talk I remember in the mid-1930's of an Indian potentate, queer for gold and ivory fittings, who put about $40,000 into the fancy body he ordered.

The last of the French-built Hispano-Suiza V-12's appeared in 1938. Over the years there had been lesser cars bearing the Hispano nameplate, notably the Junior built in the Ballot factory, which Hispano-Suiza took over in 1931. The Barcelona factory continued building cars until 1943. But none of these were supercars like the H6 or the J-12.

In 1946 or 1947 Hispano-Suiza built a prototype front-wheel-drive, independently suspended car that was to be powered by a 4-liter V-8 engine of its own make. Until such an engine could be built, a Ford V-8 was installed for test purposes. Sadly, nothing came of this project. And a few years ago the prototype was scrapped. Mark Birkigt died in 1953, but the French Hispano-Suiza company still carries on, building aircraft components, including some for the Concorde.

In 1946 the Hispano-Suiza factory in Barcelona became part of Empresa Nacional de Autocamiones S.A., which built the wonderfully exotic Pegaso sports car during the 1950's. Today E.N.A.S.A. builds excellent trucks and buses.

Between 1904 and 1943 the Spanish and French factories built some 12,000 Hispano-Suizas. A surprising number still survive, many of them reverently coddled by enthusiastic members of the Hispano-Suiza Society, of which this writer is a proud member.

Top: This 1928 H6B Hispano-Suiza, with elegant drophead coachwork by Henri Chaprou, was once owned by the Bey of Tunis. Bottom: The 1937 V-12, 11.3-liter Type 68 Bis Hispano-Suiza could perform like a sports car and accelerate from zero to 60 mph in twelve seconds.

Maserati

ention the name Maserati today and people have visions of the most dramatically configured (and very nearly the fastest) sports road express in which one might traverse the world's superhighways.

But the cars that made the name of Maserati great were not like that at all. Those early Maseratis were spartan, uncomfortable, noisy, and very rough machines, indeed.

Carolina Maserati produced the six Maserati brothers—Carlo, Bindo, Alfieri, Mario, Ettore, and Ernesto—toward the end of the nineteenth century in the north Italian town of Voghera, near Piacenza. Their father, Rudolfo Maserati, was a locomotive engineer. All of them, except Mario, who became an artist, were imbued with a love of machinery from the time they were children. But, obviously, not at the same time—the youngest of them must have still been in diapers when the eldest, by some eighteen years, began building motorcycles. By 1897 Carlo, who worked in a bicycle factory, had already built himself a belt-drive motorbike with a single-cylinder four-stroke engine.

This primitive machine so impressed a titled fellow, grandly named the Marquese Carcano di Anzano del Parco, who lived nearby, that he put up the lire to establish the boy in a motorcycle-building business. The machines were, of course, named Carcanos. Within a couple of years Carlo Maserati's Carcanos were good enough to win races. In 1900, during one of the races, the 127-mile Brescia-Mantua-Brescia race in which Carlo won the motorcycle class, he met that famous and flamboyant Fiat racing driver Vincenzo Lancia, who regaled him with the glories of the Fiat company, then still in its infancy.

So Carlo chucked the motorcycle business and, through Lancia, got a job at Fiat. Although he was still enthusiastic about racing, he had no chance to drive in competition, for Fiat already employed some of the world's great racing drivers: Nazzaro, Cagno, and, of course, Lancia. Carlo did, however, become Fiat's chief tester. Dissatisfied, he later took jobs at several other Italian car companies—there were lots of them in those days—but without much luck as a racing driver.

Carlo's brothers Alfieri and Bindo, also more than a little car crazy, went to work for Isotta Fraschini as car testers and in 1908 Alfieri, then only twenty-one, got a chance to drive the sensational little overhead-camshaft 1,200-cc Isotta FE in the Grand Prix des Voiturettes at Dieppe. Most of the competitors were those weird, long-stroked, single- and twin-cylindered French monstrosities that for a time dominated *voiturette* racing. But Alfieri didn't do too well against them, finishing fourteenth after being plagued with a malfunctioning carburetor.

Two years later the Maseratis suffered the loss of their most brilliant sibling, the

*Preceding pages: The magnificent rear-engined Bora
is the queen of the Maserati line. Its 4,719-cc V-8 engine
with quadruple overhead camshafts develops
some 335 hp at 6,000 rpm. Top speed is over 170 mph.
Although a tigress, the Bora handles like a pussycat.
The price was $36,800 the last time we asked.*

exuberant Carlo, who became ill and died in 1910. Soon afterward Alfieri and his sixteen-year-old brother Ettore were sent off to Isotta Fraschini's Buenos Aires factory. There they not only tested Isottas but also put together a racing car mostly out of Isotta Fraschini parts.

The Maserati brothers had, by now, considerable experience with every kind of motorcar, from small race cars like the tiny 1,200-cc Isotta to some of the 10-liter giants also built by Isotta. Certainly, too, they had learned a lot from the various competition machines they had constructed and from the variety of cars customers brought in to the automobile repair shop that Alfieri set up in Bologna, after leaving Argentina in 1913.

It is quite possible, too, that the Maseratis might have gone into the business of building cars, as so many of the mechanics who succeeded in raising a bit of money managed to do in northern Italy in those days. Almost-forgotten Italian makes like Chiribiri, Pavesi e Tolotti, Squillace, Revelli, Mirabilia, Ceirano come to mind. There were many, many more.

But Alfieri, Bindo, and Ettore busïed themselves with a more urgent occurrence—World War I. They worked on airplane engines at the Isotta Fraschini factory. Alfieri, who was the most experienced, worked in the engineering department on the design and improvement of the engines and soon became familiar with the most sophisticated engineering advances. Bindo and Ettore were in the production department, where they were involved with testing. As if

Alfieri weren't busy enough, he designed spark plugs that used stacks of mica washers as insulators. These he manufactured in his Bologna shop, the same shop that a decade later would be the headquarters and factory of Officine Alfieri Maserati. It would be the trident of Neptune, whose statue stood in Bologna's main square, that would ever afterward be emblazoned on Maserati cars.

After the war Giustino Cattaneo, who was Isotta Fraschini's chief engineer and a good friend of Alfieri, put the factory's facilities at his disposal so that he might get going in racing again. Alfieri built a race car with a big four-cylinder Isotta engine mounted in a cut-down chassis and with this improvised two-seater proceeded to win a couple of hill climbs and races against Fiats and Alfa Romeos.

At the time Diatto cars were still being produced. They were unexciting machines and their builders thought that racing might, somehow, give them a more sporting image. Alfieri was hired to build and race a competition car based on their best model, the 3-liter Tipo 35. He came up with a quite sleek-looking two-seater capable of some 95 mph with which he came in third overall and won the 3-liter class in the Autumn Grand Prix at Monza in 1922, beating the Alfa Romeos.

Alfieri built several other racing machines based on Diattos. He and other drivers raced these with such success that the Diatto factory's owners were moved to splurge on a Grand Prix car that Alfieri was to build from

MONACO
2 AVRIL 1934

6ème GRAND PRIX
AUTOMOBILE

the ground up. This was a supercharged twin-ohc 2-liter straight-eight clothed in a svelte racing two-seater body. It was finished so close to race time for the 1925 Italian Grand Prix at Monza that only one thin coat of Italian racing red paint could be slapped onto its aluminum body and it ran colored an Italian racing *pink*. Untested, the Diatto didn't run very long before its supercharger came adrift and its well-known driver, Emilio Materassi, had to call it quits.

Diatto called it quits, too. Racing was too expensive for them and Alfieri Maserati found himself on his own. The Grand Prix formula for 1926–1927 was limited to 1,500 cc and Alfieri reduced his engine's capacity to that size. Now the car was called the Tipo 26 Maserati—the very first Maserati—and so named it ran in its first race, the 1926 Targa Florio, that grueling contest over the miserable, climbing, twisting roads of Sicily. Alfieri drove with Guerino Bertocchi as his riding mechanic. Twenty-one cars failed to finish, but the Maserati survived to come in ninth overall and first in the 1,500-cc class.

That was but the beginning. During the next decade or so, until after the appearance in 1934 of the Germans in their almost unbeatable new Mercedes and Auto-Unions, the Maserati became one of the most successful racing machines in the world.

In 1929 a most formidable if rather dangerous Maserati made its appearance. This was the Tipo V4, or Sedici Cilindri ("sixteen cylinders"), long remembered with horror by the poor fellows who had to drive it. Two twin-ohc 2-liter eight-cylinder engines were mounted side by side on one crankcase. Each unit had a Roots blower at its nose. They blew at the fairly high pressure of 15 psi; 305 bhp at 5,200 rpm was realized. The engine was coupled to a single clutch and gearbox. The monster was capable of some 160 mph.

The Sedici Cilindri driven by the very courageous Baconin Borzacchini was timed at 152.9 mph for 10 kilometers at a race over the Circuit of Cremona in July, 1929, taking the Class F world's record. Because of mechanical problems, however, it did not finish the race. Borzacchini won the Tripoli Grand Prix in the same car.

Still, the Sedici Cilindri soon inspired Vittorio Jano to design an Alfa Romeo with twin 1,750-cc engines. It was even harder to handle because it had two clutches, two gearboxes, and two drive shafts.

The first Sedici Cilindri ended up as a sports car with a fine-looking body by Zagato. In pre-World War II days such rare conversions of racing Maseratis were the only Maserati passenger cars. For sports-car competition Maserati racing cars were fitted with fenders, lights, and windshields.

By 1930, only four years after their first appearance in top-class racing, the Maseratis were already among the most important contenders. In that year the Tipo 8C-2500 took the field. Like the earlier cars, this one had a straight-eight blown twin-ohc engine. The su-

Top: Ernesto Maserati and Guerino Bertocchi drove an 8C-2500 in the 1929 Targa Florio. Middle left: Stirling Moss and Jean Behra won the 1957 Swedish Grand Prix in a Type 450S. Middle right: 1934 poster featured a Grand Prix Maserati. Bottom: Tazio Nuvolari in a 6C/3400 Maserati at the 1934 Italian Grand Prix.

percharger took sustenance from a Weber carburetor, and a Scintilla magneto provided the sparks. At 6,000 rpm, 175 bhp was developed.

The chassis was quite conventional, with a multiple-disc clutch, a four-speed gearbox, and torque-tube drive. The frame was of simple ladder type with half-elliptic springs all around. Unfortunately, steering and roadholding were not the best.

Alfieri Maserati's old connection with Isotta Fraschini continued, for IF made many of the light alloy elektron castings for the cars. About 140 mph was possible.

Nineteen-thirty was a great year for Maserati, for the marque had, during that season, seven major victories. After several races in which the Maseratis did just so-so, Luigi Arcangeli, driving an 8C 2500, won the Rome Grand Prix, over Louis Chiron's 35B Bugatti and Nu-

volari's P2 Alfa Romeo. Alfieri Maserati won the 1,100-cc class.

Oddly, in that same year, a Sedici Cilindri was entered at Indianapolis. But blowers had been banned and Borzacchini had to drive without them. He soon quit with engine trouble.

After some minor wins, the big event was the Monza Grand Prix in September. The race was peculiarly divided into heats for the various classes.

In the 2,000–3,000-cc heat, the Maseratis driven by Luigi Arcangeli, Luigi Fagioli, and Achille Varzi outran the 35B Bugattis and P2 Alfas driven by such cracks as Borzacchini, Campari, and Nuvolari. Even the Sedici Cilindri driven by Ernesto Maserati won its heat against Rudolf Caracciola's huge Mercedes-Benz and Babe Stapp's American Duesenberg.

The final heat was a runaway for the Maseratis of Varzi, Arcangeli, and Ernesto Maserati. By 1930 the newcomer Maserati was right up there with the best racing machines in the world. It was not only the equal of the 35B Bugattis and P2 Alfa Romeos, it was, at least in 1930, their superior.

In the years to come Maserati had its ups and downs. Its competitors became harder to defeat. Alfa Romeo fielded its Monzas and Monoposto P-3's, Bugatti brought out the twin-cam Type 51, then the fast but unwieldy Type 54, and finally the beautiful 3.3-liter Type 59. Although Maserati's Tipo 8C-3000, the 230-bhp Tipo 8CM, a new 5-liter Sedici Cilindri, and the V-8 R1 were hard pressed, they continued to win races, especially when Tazio Nuvolari was the driver.

Alfieri Maserati had undoubtedly led his brothers into such greatness. Without him there would have been no Maserati cars, no Maserati racing team. In 1932 he died after an operation necessitated by an injury he had received in a racing accident some five years earlier. His death was a serious setback to the Officine Maserati, but by 1932 the company, led by Alfieri's surviving brothers, was strong enough to proceed without him.

In 1934 the Mercedes and Auto-Unions appeared and within a year, after they got over their teething troubles, other Grand Prix cars rarely won a race against them.

In 1938 Officine Alfieri Maserati was added to the industrial empire of the very rich Orsi family of Modena. They were interested in taking over not only the racing-car operation, but also the successful spark-plug business. The Orsi outfit was headed by Commendatore Adolfo Orsi, and his son Omer became head of Maserati, which was moved from Bologna to Modena. The three Maserati brothers contracted to stay with Orsi for ten years.

The first fruit of the Orsi regime was the Tipo 8CTF, which had a straight-eight twin-ohc engine with two superchargers. It put out 360 bhp at 6,000 rpm. The 8CTF did only fairly well in Europe, but it was remarkably successful at Indianapolis. Wilbur Shaw twice won the 500 in 8CTF Maseratis suitably disguised as Boyle Specials.

Even the 360-hp 8CTF wasn't competitive against the Mercedes and Auto-Unions. By the late thirties Maserati, like Alfa Romeo, was concentrating on *voiturette* racing in 1,500-cc cars like the 6CM with its 4-cylinder supercharged twin-ohc engine, which was often trounced by the tall, ungainly-looking British E.R.A.'s.

After World War II Maserati plunged into racing again. Their Grand Prix cars of many different configurations and driven by champions like Stirling Moss and Juan Fangio gave their chief contenders, the Ferraris, a very hard time, indeed. And Maseratis also became preeminent in sports-car racing.

Unlike Alfa Romeo and Ferrari, Maserati had not deigned to produce sports and Gran Turismo cars for the public to buy. But

Top: 1948 Pinin Farina-bodied Type A6G Maserati
had a six-cylinder, 1,500-cc engine that developed
65 hp. Its top speed was 90 mph. Bottom: This
1964 3500 GTIS Sebring with body by Vignale had a
six-cylinder, 3,700-cc engine developing 235 hp.
Top speed was about 140 mph.

179

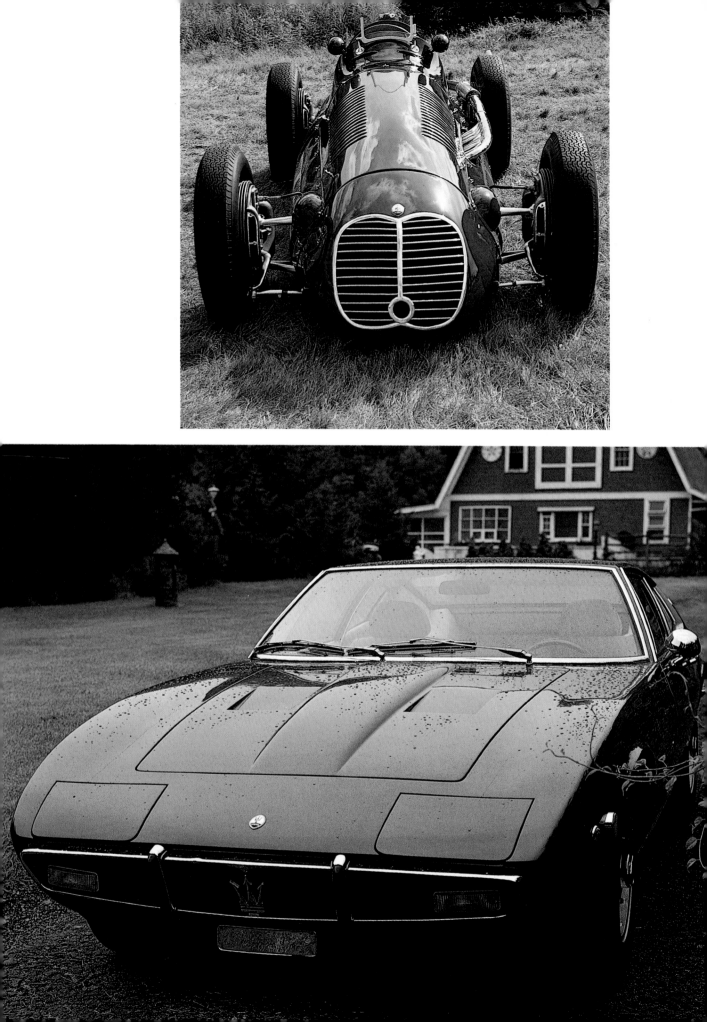

the Orsi management aimed to change this situation. As early as 1948 a Pinin Farina-bodied GT car was shown at the Turin show, but this prototype, the A6G, with a six-cylinder 1½-liter engine that put out some 65 bhp, didn't actually go into series production. Starting in 1954, a few A6GCS's with 1,500-cc six-cylinder engines, as well as the A6G 2000, were built in small numbers with bodies by Zagato, Frua, and Pinin Farina. (The A6G 2000 was later called the A6G/54.)

But it wasn't until 1958 that Maserati actually started building sports and GT cars in any numbers. Its first Gran Turismo car was the very potent 3500 GT, of which some two thousand examples were built between 1958 and 1964.

The 3500 GT's engine was a six with twin overhead camshafts and three double-choke Weber carburetors. It was based on the engine in the car driven by Stirling Moss in the 1956 Mille Miglia. Although detuned, the production engine put out 230 bhp at 5,500 rpm. Top speed was about 145 mph—quick for the fifties. The bodies by Touring, Allemano, and other top Italian coachbuilders were mounted on complex space frames. At first disc brakes were used only up front. Later versions had them all around. After 1962 fuel injection was available on the GTI model.

The brutal 5000 GT's engine was based on that in the 450S sports-racing machine that Fangio and Moss had campaigned in 1957. It was a V-8 with quadruple overhead camshafts that developed no less than 350 hp at 6,000 rpm, even after it had been defanged and quieted down (slightly) for street use. It was mounted in the same frame used in the 3500 GT. Only about thirty of these overly muscular monsters were ever built, but the design of its engine lived on in the later Ghibli and Bora models.

I must admit that the GT Maserati model I've always liked best was the Mistral, which first appeared in 1965. It's a nice, simple-looking machine, handy, with a short 96-inch wheelbase—the kind police don't look at more than twice. But its 4,014-cc six-cylinder engine (early Mistrals had 3,692-cc engines) gives it more than enough verve—255 bhp at 5,500 rpm and a top speed of over 150 mph. A good friend owns one and I'm always happy to drive it.

One Maserati GT car always left me cold. This was the Ghibli, which came out in 1966. Although it had a quite short 102-inch wheelbase, its long overhangs fore and aft made it look too long, too sleek, too much the expensive promenade car for rich doctors and dentists. (A Maserati dealer once told me he sold many of them to such medical types.) Still, its super-smooth skin, designed by Giorgetto Giugiario and built by Ghia, hid tigerish machinery. For the Ghibli was powered by a 4,935-cc V-8 engine with four overhead camshafts. It developed 355 bhp at 5,500 rpm. Its chassis was surprisingly old fashioned with a solid rear axle hung on semielliptic springs. Although the factory claimed that a Ghibli could be pushed along at some 174 mph I suspect that this number was

Top: 1948 4 CLT/48 Maserati Grand Prix machine had a 1,489-cc supercharged four-cylinder engine that developed 260 hp. Its top speed was 156 mph. Bottom: Maserati Ghibli with rain-spattered hood. This car's 4,935-cc V-8 engine puts out 355 hp; top speed is some 174 mph. Giorgetto Giugiario designed the body.

something for Ghibli owners to mention at cocktail parties.

The Indy, which first appeared in 1969, also had a live rear axle on semielliptic springs. With a similar 4.9-liter engine, it was just about as fast as the Ghibli. But it was unique in that it could transport four passengers in high-speed, if not exactly quiet, luxury.

The Indy came out soon after Citroën got control of Maserati. But things weren't that simple. For Citroën in turn, was then owned by Michelin and Fiat. Further, Fiat owned a big piece of Ferrari.

Citroën wanted Maserati in order to acquire a source of high-quality, high-potency, six-cylinder engines for its new luxury car, the 1970 Citroën SM, a very fine machine in which everything worked hydropneumatically—suspension, brakes, steering, seat adjustment—everything. The SM, sadly, is no more. But some of its sophisticated entrails still function in present-day Maseratis.

You might imagine that any car Maserati might produce after becoming part of that Franco-Italian complex would be a typical corporate compromise. Instead, Maserati gave birth to the greatest GT machine ever to bear the trident—the superb Bora.

The Bora was a sensation when it was first shown at Geneva in 1972. And rightly so. For this mid-engined machine designed by Maserati's chief engineer, Giulio Alfieri, and styled by Giugiario was, and still is, unique, not only in its look but also in its performance.

The engine, which lives behind the two seats of the Bora, is a 4,719-cc V-8 with quadruple overhead camshafts and four Weber carburetors. It develops 335 bhp at 6,000 rpm, enough to rush the car along at some 170 mph. Power is transmitted by a ZF five-speed gearbox. Suspension is, of course, independent front and rear. Steering is by rack and pinion. The Girling ventilated disc brakes are applied by the hydropneumatic system inherited from Citroën, which also works the faired-in disappearing headlights, the seat and steering-wheel adjustments, and the ingenious system that moves the pedals in and out. No matter how a Bora's driver is constructed—short with long gorillalike arms or tall and long-legged with short arms—he'll quickly adjust things to fit him with perfection.

On occasion I've been lucky enough to have been allowed to drive a Bora. Although I've never been brave enough to approach its top speed nor to test its limits of adhesion, no liberties I took with it—and they were more daring than anything I had ever attempted in any other car—gave me the feeling that I was getting in over my head.

The last time I took one out I found myself early one morning on a very twisting, downhill road in northwestern Connecticut. Normally I'd frighten myself negotiating such a rotten piece of road-engineering at 60 mph. My passenger quietly murmured that I was exceeding 80. And he was able to merely murmur because, although the engine was close behind us, we moved in smooth silence. We took badly

Top: The Type 109 GTI Mistral's drophead body was built by Vignale. The 4-liter engine put out 255 hp; top speed was 150 mph. Bottom: The V-6 rear-engined 150-mph Merak/SS is Maserati's "economy" version of the Bora. It costs only $27,620. Note that the rear-end treatment of the body is unlike the Bora's.

cambered short-radius turns with no squealing, no sliding. The brakes, the five-speed gearbox were so very good, so viceless, as to be almost unnoticed. On a straight stretch of two-lane road, other traffic could almost be ignored, for with the Bora's fierce acceleration there was no drama involved during passing at high speed. After all, a Bora will reach 80 in under ten seconds, 100 in about fifteen seconds.

But you have to pay for such high-speed magnificence. A Bora sells for $36,800 in the United States.

If $36,800 (plus dealer preparation and freight) seems a bit much, you can buy an economy model, the Merak/SS, for only $27,620. This svelte sister of the Bora, which it very strongly resembles, has a different rear-window treatment with a rear deck plus a pair of flying buttresses that flow rearward from the roof. It has no quarter windows like those of the Bora.

The Merak/SS hasn't quite the muscle of the Bora, since it is propelled by an enlarged version of the V-6 engine that once powered the Citroën SM. This 2,965-cc four-ohc engine now puts out 220 bhp at 6,500 rpm and 150 mph is claimed by the factory. Otherwise the Merak/SS is much like the Bora except that it is lighter—by almost 1,000 pounds.

Corporate catastrophes in 1975 almost put an end to the production of Maseratis. Peugeot had taken over ailing Citroën. The Modena factory, which had been much enlarged to build the engines for the Citroën SM, was

closed and its work force laid off. But that mover and shaker, Alejandro de Tomaso, who had once raced Maseratis and who had built the de Tomaso Pantera which, for a time, had been marketed by Ford, would not allow the marque to disappear. He took over Maserati. So the Bora, the Merak/SS, the front-engined 4.9-liter Khamsin, and the four-passenger Kyalami are still being built, albeit in small numbers.

The trident of Bologna still cleaves the wind on the prows of proud motorcars.

Top: This front-engined 4.9-liter Maserati
Khamsin 2 + 2 coupe was designed by Bertone. The V-8
engine develops 320 hp, and the car will reach
170 mph. A Khamsin costs about $40,000. Bottom: Designer
Giorgetto Giugiario's elegant treatment of
the rear deck of the Maserati Bora.

"One never *drives* one. It simply isn't done!" The stuffy character who uttered this dictum must have been talking about that most chic of aristocratic conveyances, the straight-eight 8B Isotta Fraschini, whose front seats were most suitably occupied by a liveried chauffeur and a footman. The owner would no more drive his Isotta than he would handle the throttle of the Pacific locomotive hauling the *Flèche d'Or* express toward Paris.

Certainly, some Isottas were fitted with two-seated convertible bodies of surpassing arrogance. But these were for the kinds of people whose egos required that they drive a conveyance that took some 3 tons of machinery mounted on a chassis with no less than 146 inches of wheelbase to transport the driver and his single passenger. They sat behind a hood that stretched for some 7 feet between radiator and windshield.

The grandiose 8B of 1930–1932 was the last of a long line of Isotta Fraschinis (we'll have a bit more to say about it farther on), for the marque was born some thirty years earlier, in 1901, when Cesare Isotta and Oreste Fraschini exhibited a single-cylindered 5-hp horseless carriage in Milan.

Signori Isotta and Fraschini, youthful members of the Milanese upper crust, had driven various motor vehicles—Benzes, De Dion tricycles, Renaults—before the turn of the century. In 1900 the newly formed firm of Isotta Fraschini became the Italian representative of Renault and started to import the company's 3½-hp model. With its shaft drive and front-mounted engine, the Renault was no longer a gas buggy like so many of its contemporaries—especially the behind-the-times German Benz, which, until IF started to bring in Renaults, was the most popular of the few cars in Milan.

Soon Isotta Fraschini, in order to reduce customs charges, began to assemble the little Renaults from parts, since the duty on bits and pieces was less than that on complete cars. Bodywork was built in Milan. As often happens when cars are assembled far from their birthplaces, changes in design started to creep in. Soon Isotta Fraschini installed 8- and 10-hp Aster engines in their versions of the Renaults, whose standard power plant was the De Dion-Bouton because the company did not yet build its own engines.

By 1904 Isotta Fraschini was building its own line of cars designed by Giuseppe Stefanini. These had 12-hp, four-cylinder engines, pressed-steel chassis frames, and chain drive. Things moved fast in those days, and by 1906 Isotta Fraschinis were becoming surprisingly muscular, especially after the arrival in 1905 of the remarkable Giustino Cattaneo, who for almost thirty years was chief designer, plant manager, and managing director. Over the years the energetic and eminently likable Cattaneo designed and produced thirty-six models of I-

Preceding pages: Imposing frontal aspect
of the 1929 Tipo 8A Isotta Fraschini Castagna-bodied
convertible coupe. The straight-eight, 7,370-cc
engine developed 115 bhp. Such grandiose chariots were
built with the rich American market in mind.
Note the beautifully complex Grebel headlights.

sotta Fraschini, as well as many marine engines, aero engines, military vehicles, and World War I tanks.

It was fashionable in the early 1900's for car manufacturers to ape the highly successful Mercedes, and Isotta-Fraschini was no exception. The honeycomb radiator, chain drive, and transmission brake were all part of the Isotta's specifications. Only the peculiar Mercedes "scroll" clutch, wherein a spring gripped the drive shaft, was eschewed by IF in favor of a more normal cone clutch.

Various sizes of Isotta were offered by 1906, from a 4-liter, four-cylinder model to a brute of a 10½-liter machine. All of them, of course, were luxury cars meant either for export or for the minuscule rich upper class of Italy. For Italy, unlike Britain, France, or the United States, had almost no financially comfortable middle class.

Isotta Fraschinis were raced from the very beginning. Even the Isotta-assembled Renaults of 1900 had appeared on the race courses. In 1905, the same year in which Cattaneo joined the company and a huge new factory on the via Monterosa in Milan was finished, Isotta Fraschini decided to get into big-time racing as Fiat had. Stefanini therefore designed a typical saurian monster of the period, the huge 100-hp Tipo D with a four-cylinder engine that displaced no less than 17 liters. Remarkably, Stefanini had provided an overhead camshaft driven by a vertical shaft to operate its valves. Although it was considered revolutionary at the time, the American Welch of 1904 had not only such a shaft-driven camshaft above its cylinders, but also inclined valves and hemispherical combustion chambers. The Isotta's valves were vertical. Sadly, the 100-hp Tipo D didn't fare very well in the Italian Coppa Florio race of September, 1905. One car, driven by Vincenzo Trucco, failed in practice. Another, driven by Frenchman Hubert Le Blon, barely completed one lap before its flywheel fell off. But the D had started a tradition of overhead camshafts in Isotta racing and sporting machines. Further, the Tipo D was the last purely racing machine built by IF. Later racing cars, even those that ran in the Indianapolis 500 in 1913, were developed from passenger and sports cars available to the public. It was through its successes in racing, not only in Europe with European drivers, but in places as far away as Savannah, Georgia, Briarcliff, New York, and Bridgeport, Connecticut, where the cars were driven by Americans like Al Poole and Lewis Strang, that Isotta Fraschini became a notable name in the years before the Kaiser War.

In 1908 Isotta Fraschini entered a car in the Grand Prix des Voiturettes at Dieppe that would become the progenitor of almost every small, agile sports car built during the next seventy years. This was the Tipo FE, which had a four-cylinder monobloc engine of only 1,200 cc. Designed by Stefanini, it had an overhead camshaft, vertical valves, and hemispherical combustion chambers. Its wheelbase was only 83 inches and it weighed little more than 1,500 pounds. Top speed was 56 mph.

*Driver and passenger sat a long distance aft
of the prow of the Tipo 8A Isotta Fraschini. The long
hood accommodated the huge engine, which could
propel the heavy machine at almost 90 mph. With
luxurious coachwork by Castagna, such an Isotta cost
some $25,000 delivered in the United States.*

The tiny FE's, including one driven by Alfieri Maserati, then a mere beginner at racing, did not win that *voiturette* race. The best that one of them could do was eighth place. (Maserati had carburetor trouble and came in fourteenth.) The winner was one of those weird, ultra-long-stroked, single-cylindered Delages.

But the tiny FE caused such a furor that a less sporting version, complete with top and, if desired, a windshield, was offered. This was called the FENC, and it was slightly slower than the FE, being capable of 47 mph.

The FE's were so Bugatti-ish in concept that it was long thought that Ettore Bugatti had been involved in their design. This view was reinforced by the fact that the firm of Lorraine-Dietrich had controlled Isotta Fraschini from 1907 until 1911. And Bugatti had once freelanced for them. But we now know that Ettore had nothing to do with the FE. In fact, it is possible that the FE inspired Bugatti's later designs. Further, Bugatti, not a man to hide his successes, would certainly have let it be known that the FE was one of his illegitimate children.

It was not only the FE that made 1908 a great year for IF. In that year Isotta Fraschini also won the Targa Florio in Sicily, and Herbert Lytle, behind the wheel of a comparatively small-engined, 50-hp IF, finished second behind George Robertson's big Locomobile in the Vanderbilt Cup race on Long Island.

Before World War I almost forty different models of Isotta Fraschini came out of the doors of the big via Monterosa factory. Only the FE and FENC were small and agile machines. Most were rather dull, if superbly constructed, midsized, four-cylinder, T-head- and L-head-engined cars of splendid utility, if not overly romantic. A notable few, however, made up for their rather prosaic sisters.

There was nothing ordinary about the lovely ugly monster, the 1914 Tipo KM, in which its owner Austin Clark once invited me to accompany him. The elephantine KM was more car than any I have ever climbed aboard. It seemed, somehow, even bigger and bulkier than its 130-inch wheelbase and 5,000-pound weight might lead one to expect. Although the KM was a clumsy machine with heavy, not-too-precise steering, it didn't appear to give Clark any trouble, for he almost immediately took it up to about 80 mph, close to the KM's top speed. At that speed the engine seemed to be merely idling, for it was only doing some 1,600 rpm.

Such rapid progression worried me a little, for we were threading our way through a fair amount of Long Island traffic and depending on 1913-type brakes. True, the KM had four-wheel brakes, but, as Clark pointed out, their powers of retardation were not much better than the two-wheel brakes fitted on other 1914 machines. The brakes were arranged in a most peculiar way. There were two pedals for Clark to push: one applied the rear-wheel brakes, the other a brake on the transmission. To use the front-wheel brakes, which the KM catalog referred to as "emergency brakes," Clark had to pull hard on a big outside lever.

The four-cylinder KM engine displaced no less than 10,618 cc (130-mm bore x 200-mm stroke). *Each* cylinder had a cubic capacity of over 2,650 cc, twice that of the entire engine in the X1-9 Fiat my wife drives. An overhead camshaft, driven by a vertical shaft at the front of the engine, operated four valves per cylinder. The valves were in removable cages. At a mere 1,600 rpm, 140 hp was generated. Oddly, in order to save a little weight, the bucket-sized pistons were bored with lightening holes. A high-tension Bosch magneto driven by the same vertical shaft that was geared to the camshaft supplied the sparks. Full-pressure lubrication was used.

A multiple-disc clutch, a four-speed gearbox, and double side chains inside cases that held lubricant transmitted power to the rear wheels. Clark's car ran on ugly spoked steel wheels, but wire wheels could be substituted.

Tipo KM's invariably had open bodies. Some cars were delivered with pear-shaped radiator shells. Later models sported sharply pointed prows à la Mercedes.

The Tipo IM of 1913 was not only a supersporting Isotta Fraschini, it also ran as a racing car at Indianapolis in 1913 and 1914. It was built to satisfy the importunities of Isotta's American agents, who hoped that racing publicity might help sales. A smaller version of the mighty KM, it was no slouch in the speed department, for it was about as fast. As a touring car it was capable of 80 mph. In Indianapolis form it could reach 95 or so.

A few years ago I had the chance to examine the beautifully restored example that William P. Snyder brought to the big antique car meet at Hershey, Pennsylvania. The overhead-camshaft four-cylinder engine of the IM looked much like that of the KM, but it was smaller: 7,238 cc (120 x 160 mm). The IM engine revved a little faster, too—2,200 rpm. In Indy form it revved at 2,350 rpm. Standard horsepower was 120; Indy horsepower, 135. Its four-wheel braking system was a bit different from the Tipo KM's. It had but one brake pedal, which applied the rear-wheel brakes. The outside hand-brake lever put on the front-wheel brakes.

Cattaneo had experimented with four-wheel brakes as early as 1909 and the KM and IM cars were the first anywhere to have such anchors. Certainly, other designers had unsuccessfully grappled with the problem, notably the engineers at Daimler in England in 1906. The Scottish Argyll boasted four-wheel brakes in 1911. But such stoppers were an exception until after World War I. Until then four-wheel brakes were considered highly dangerous. Rolls-Royce, for example, had rear-wheel-only brakes on their Silver Ghost until 1924.

Sadly, the Isotta Fraschini IM's did very poorly at Indianapolis in 1913 and 1914. Sports cars with high centers of gravity and old-fashioned chain drives, and merely disguised as racers with pointy-tailed two-seater bodies, they hadn't a chance against American cars like the Duesenberg-built Masons and Mercers or the foreign Peugeots, Sunbeams, and Mercedes.

Top: 1908 Tipo FE racing voiturette had a 1,200-cc, four-cylinder engine. Middle: Herbert Lytle on the Isotta Fraschini that finished second in 1908 Vanderbilt Cup Race. Bottom: 1913 sporting Tipo IM and 110-hp overhead camshaft engine also used in IM race cars.

Top: Londoners gape at the 1912 Tipo OM
25/35-hp Isotta Fraschini, which had a four-cylinder
engine, four-wheel brakes, and chain drive.
Bottom: The ill-fated 1947 Monterosa prototype had a
rear-mounted V-8 3.4-liter engine. The last
of the Isottas, it never went into production.

The only reason they were entered at all was that Isotta's American agents insisted they be. They also paid all the bills. In 1913 Harry Grant, Teddy Tetzlaff, and Isotta factory driver Vincenzo Trucco drove the Isottas. All three retired. Jules Goux won on a Peugeot. Spencer Wishart's Mercer was second.

In 1914 only one Isotta Fraschini IM was entered. This was driven by my old friend, the late Ray Gilhooley, who then performed the famous spin that still carries his name. The accident was caused by a broken drive chain, and poor Ray bore the scar it gave him for the rest of his life. A Delage driven by René Thomas won. Arthur Duray's Peugeot was second.

During World War I, which Italy entered in 1915, Isotta Fraschini, like every other automobile maker, was involved with building military hardware. Besides trucks and armored cars, Isotta Fraschini built thousands of marine and airplane engines. These were nothing new to Isotta, for Cattaneo had experimented with airplane engines as early as 1908.

Despite involvement with war work, Cattaneo's engineers continued to experiment with new types of automobile, especially with straight eights. When the war ended, Isotta Fraschini decided that instead of spreading itself over many models, it would build only one, a superluxury car. Like Rolls-Royce and Hispano-Suiza, Isotta would cater to the new millionaires. Especially those in the United States.

The new Tipo 8 Isotta Fraschini was announced in August, 1919. It was the world's first production car with a straight-eight engine. Compared with some previous Isottas, the engine's capacity was moderate: 5,902 cc. Its block was cast aluminum with steel cylinder liners. The valves, two per cylinder, were operated by pushrods and rockers. Compression ratio was a mere 5 to 1. The long, long crankshaft revolved on nine main bearings. Only some 75 bhp was developed at 2,200 rpm. A multiple-disc clutch, a three-speed gearbox with a centrally placed gear lever without a visible gate, and a torque tube to the 3.75-to-1 spiral-bevel rear end comprised the drive line.

The 146-inch-wheelbase chassis was distressingly ordinary, with a ladder-type frame and semielliptic springs all around. Its four-wheel brakes were helped by a servo. Every part of the car was constructed and finished to remarkably high standards. With the kinds of heavy, luxury limousine bodies it was meant to haul around, a Tipo 8 couldn't do much better than 70 mph. With an open body it could approach 80 or so. A Tipo 8 was no ball of fire, but it wasn't meant to be. Its role was to quietly transport the rich in formal luxury.

Still, the Isotta was faster and more modern than the Edwardian Silver Ghost Rolls-Royce, which was still in production. Its other competitor for the custom of the moneyed, the H6 Hispano-Suiza, made the Isotta look like the klutz it was. The Hispano, with its slightly larger 6.6-liter overhead-camshaft engine, was quicker, lighter, and handled better, though its overhead camshaft made it slightly noisier.

The Tipo 8 was superseded by the 8A in 1924. It was hoped that the new model would prove to be as quick and maneuverable as the H6B Hispano-Suiza and would therefore capture some of the Hispano's customers. Earlier a special sports model of the Tipo 8, the Spinto, had been brought out to challenge the Hispano. But it had failed to do so. The cubic capacity of the 8A was increased to 7,370 cc and horsepower was raised to 115 bhp at 2,400 rpm. Brakes were improved and a Dewandre vacuum brake booster fitted. Tires were fatter.

Still, the 8A was no match for a Hispano-Suiza until the Super Spinto model—the 8 ASS of 1926—appeared. This version had slightly more compression—5.5 to 1—bigger valves, double valve springs, and dual-downdraft carburetors, each with its own manifold. The factory guaranteed 100 mph from its 150 bhp. It was said to accelerate from zero to 80 mph in twenty-five seconds.

The 8A was still in production when the Depression dried up the sales of such big baubles. After all, an Isotta cost about $25,000 delivered in New York in 1929. And some with particularly fancy coachwork cost rather more— one, replete with silver and ivory fittings, was said to have cost $40,000.

The Tipo 8B of 1931 was the last of the Isotta Fraschini battleships. Instead of being cast in aluminum, the engine block was now of nickel steel. The intake manifolds were exhaust-gas heated. Twin exhaust manifolds were fitted. Coil ignition supplanted the magneto, and the crankshaft was beefed up. The buyer could choose either a synchromesh gearbox or a self-changing Wilson preselector. Toward the end the preselector gearbox was standard.

The chassis frame was redesigned for greater rigidity with deeper side members and massive cross members. Although heavier— the chassis alone weighed 3,300 pounds—the Tipo 8B was a livelier machine than the older members of the Tipo 8 family. One hundred mph was possible from the 160 bhp the engine developed at a mere 3,000 rpm. In the early 1930's Isotta Fraschini was quite as prestigious a name as Rolls-Royce and Hispano-Suiza. Still, despite the greatly improved performance of the Tipo 8B, the V-12 Hispano-Suiza and the Phantom II Rolls-Royce were formidable competitors, especially the brilliant Hispano. But even these magnificent contenders for the patronage of the ultrarich were having hard times.

I drove an 8A but once. In 1934 or so. I had bought a used 22/90 3-liter Alfa Romeo from a reputedly slippery character in 1932. I enjoyed that Alfa, and despite murmurings from friends who knew its vendor, I had a valid title to it. One Saturday morning the doorman of the apartment house in which I lived called me on the intercom and excitedly told me that some gentlemen in an "If" (his reading of the IF nameplate) wished to see me.

At the curb stood as marvelous a motorcar as I'd ever seen. It was a superbly svelte, close-coupled, four-passenger, boat-tailed, dual-cowl tourer with varnished wood decking and fenders that flared like wings. I still remember its deep blue mirrorlike flanks. I've never since seen a more perfect finish.

At the wheel sat the man who'd sold me the Alfa. A darkly handsome gentleman sat behind the rear windshield.

"Hop in, Ralph," said the man at the wheel. Dazed with the Isotta's magnificence, I obeyed. "How'd you like to own this baby?"

I laughed, "I can't afford anything like this."

"We need money fast, Aldo and me, and we'll sell this boat real cheap," he said in a confidential whisper. "But try it first."

"How much?" I asked.

"Try it first."

I suspected that he and Aldo didn't own the Isotta. It was said that on occasion my friend sold the cars people brought to his shop for repair, but I couldn't resist his offer.

That Isotta—a Super Spinto sports version of the 8A—was no slouch. I took it down Riverside Drive, then through Central Park. It steered and handled in a most lovely way (although sitting some 7 feet from the Lalique glass radiator ornament put me off a bit), and it accelerated quite as well as my Alfa. The preselector Wilson box with which I'd not yet had any experience worked sweetly. You had merely to move a lever on a quadrant on the steering column to the number of the gear you might next require. If you were running in, say, top gear you'd preselect third. Then when you wanted third speed you merely kicked what

would normally be a clutch pedal and the box changed down automatically.

The view under the hood was too simple, too neat. That big, beautifully finished straight-eight engine sat there monolithically, like a tombstone, and gave no evidence that it was running. It neither vibrated nor made a sound. Only the fan moved.

How much did my man want for this jewel? Four hundred dollars. I still chide myself for not buying the car.

Who was Aldo? He was the mechanic who'd tuned my Alfa before I'd bought it. But I hadn't at first recognized him shaved and in a very good suit.

A few months later my friend was in jail for selling a Rolls-Royce that someone had brought into the shop for Aldo to tune. And what happened to Aldo? He became the American agent for an expensive foreign sports car.

The memorably magnificent body on that Isotta tourer was typical of those on most chassis of the marque. Neither Rolls-Royce nor Hispano-Suiza and certainly not Mercedes-Benz was ever clothed in better-designed or better-built coachwork. The Carrozzeria Italiana Cesare Sala, Carrozzeria Farina, Carrozzeria Castagna, and Carrozzeria Touring in Italy, Hooper and Gurney Nutting in Britain, Figoni et Falaschi in France, and even Fleetwood in the United States built bodies of unparalleled elegance for the Isotta Fraschini.

But elegance had few buyers during the economic storm of the 1930's. Anyhow, the

The Tipo Targa Florio Isotta Fraschini not
only won the Sicilian Targa Florio race in 1908, but also
took second place in America's Vanderbilt Cup.
Its 8-liter, 70-hp, four-cylinder engine
gave a top speed of 81 mph. Note the brake and gear
levers, with holes drilled in them to cut weight.

sale of cars had by then become secondary, for Isotta Fraschini was already a very important producer of aero engines. Only fifteen Tipo 8A and Tipo 8B Isotta Fraschinis were sold in 1932. During World War II ten thousand workers at Isotta Fraschini built aero engines, trucks, aircraft machine guns, and antiaircraft cannon.

In 1947 at the Paris salon it seemed as if there might be a renaissance of the once-great Isotta Fraschini. A prototype of the new 8C Monterosa was shown. This machine had a 3.4-liter, single-ohc, V-8 engine mounted in the rear, independent suspension, and a surpass-ingly ugly bulbous body on its long, 122½-inch-wheelbase chassis. It was hoped that it might be sold in the United States, where its proponents imagined that everyone was rich.

My friend, the late great motoring journalist Laurence Pomeroy, Jr., got a chance to drive one. He told me that it went very well, was capable of close to 100 mph, and displayed no roadholding vices despite its heavy engine being hung so far astern. A dozen or so proto-type models were built, but the Monterosa never went into production.

Today an Italian government-controlled outfit with the resounding name of Fab-brica Automobili Isotta Fraschini & Motori Breda Spa. makes diesel engines, torque con-verters, and similar devices. The only connec-tion between this establishment and the old Isot-ta Fraschini company, which became insolvent in 1953, is that old IF insignia. The new engines are still so emblazoned.

Rolls-Royce

No name borne by a motorcar has the éclat, panache, prestige, and mystique of those two words, "Rolls-Royce." And this international respect and reverence for the marque has lasted these seventy-odd years. Most motorcars take a long time to achieve greatness, but the Rolls-Royce was an almost instant success. Born in 1904, it was already famous by 1907 and was soon "the Best Car in the World." We cannot think of any mechanical artifact that has for so long been considered the very model of perfection. Manufacture a superior device and it will be dubbed "the Rolls-Royce of Lawn Mowers" or "the Rolls-Royce of Pepper Mills." We've even heard of "the Rolls-Royce of Mousetraps."

Frederick Henry Royce, born in 1863, was a man of the Victorian Age. And his Rolls-Royce car (albeit first constructed three years into the reign of Edward VII) was built in the idiom of that era of meticulous mechanical construction by craftsmen who slaved for long hours at near-starvation wages. Royce himself was long used to such industrial slavery when at the age of forty he decided to build an automobile.

An orphan at nine, he had been a newsboy, a telegraph messenger, and a bound apprentice in the locomotive shops of the Great Northern Railway, where he became a fine machinist. Still, when he left the railway shops in 1880 all he could earn was eleven shillings for a fifty-four-hour week in a Leeds toolmaking factory.

But Royce was tougher than most people of his class and had the fortitude to spend what little time he had after work to learn something of what was then known of the new science of electricity. A new company, the Electric Light and Power Company in London, advertised for a tester and Royce had enough nerve to invest his savings in a third-class ticket to London to try for the job. He was hired.

Royce did well at the electric-light company and despite long hours at the powerhouse found time to take courses in electrical theory at the Polytechnic Institute in London. He soon impressed his bosses enough for them to promote him to First Electrician at their Liverpool subsidiary—the Lancashire Maxim and Western Electric Company.

Although the light bulb was invented by Sir Joseph Wilson Swan in England, it was in America that the first practical and successful power company was established by Thomas A. Edison. For some reason the various small English companies couldn't make a go of selling electric power. The Victorian English, perhaps fearful of the mysteries of electricity, still preferred gaslight. The Lancashire Maxim and Western Electric Company went bust.

Royce was out of a job again. But he wasn't worried. He'd saved £20, and at twenty he considered himself quite the electrical expert. He had an even wealthier friend, A. E. Clare-

Preceding pages: Edwardian elegance plus utility.
Enthusiastic balloonist Charles Rolls had a 1907 Rolls-Royce
Silver Ghost like this specially designed to
transport his balloon and its basket, which rode
neatly on the rear deck. With aeronautical impedimenta
removed, the rear seat could be unfolded.

mont, who possessed £50. He too was fascinated by electricity. With their £70 they set up in business in Manchester as makers of electrical devices, grandly styling themselves F. H. Royce and Company.

There wasn't too much call for electrical parts in 1884. Royce and Claremont just about kept themselves from starving by making sockets and other small parts for bigger operators. Things became slightly better after Royce designed an electric doorbell that, complete with pushbutton and wire (but without a battery), could be sold for a shilling and sixpence (thirty-seven cents!). A few pence in profit was made.

Henry Royce was a young man who lived for work. Regular hours, regular meals meant nothing to him. A sandwich, a bite of sausage could sustain him for an eighteen-hour stretch at his workbench. He experimented and read and found ways to improve the crude electrical apparatus of the time. By 1891 he had found a way to build dynamos and motors that didn't revolve in a Fourth of July shower of sparks caused by the little bundles of copper wire—the "brushes" (a term we still use)—which not only quickly burned themselves useless but also burned the rotating commutators. His sparkless dynamos and motors could now be used in explosive atmospheres where the usual pyrotechnical motors were dangerous.

The new Royce motors and dynamos were quickly successful and the little firm started to grow. In 1894 it was incorporated as "Royce Ltd. Electrical and Mechanical Engineers and Manufacturers of Dynamos, Motors and Kindred Articles." Now, too, Royce Ltd. started to manufacture a line of beautifully constructed electrically powered cranes and hoists that brought in some £20,000 ($100,000) a year by the turn of the century.

But soon the rosy glow started to dim a little. The end of the Boer War brought on a recession. German and American competitors began to undercut Royce's prices. Further, Henry Royce's health was showing the effects of his years of eighteen-hour days. His doctor and Claremont hoped that outdoor activity would revitalize him. To that end, all three bought De Dion Quadricycles—machines that would give them rather more outdoor exercise than they had bargained for.

The De Dion Quadricycle was a most peculiar self-propelled machine that looked like a pair of bicycles joined like Siamese twins. An energetic, single-cylinder engine was geared directly to the rear wheels without benefit of clutch. A minuscule brake would, it was hoped, slow it down if not actually stop it. This assumed that the machine could first be prevailed upon to start. Starting could be accomplished either by frantic pedaling or by vigorously pushing the little beast and jumping aboard.

The De Dion certainly gave Royce plenty of exercise if he could be cajoled into leaving his work. But he persisted in his long hours and eventually broke down. His doctor and Claremont forced him to take a sea voyage—the cure for everything in those days—and he

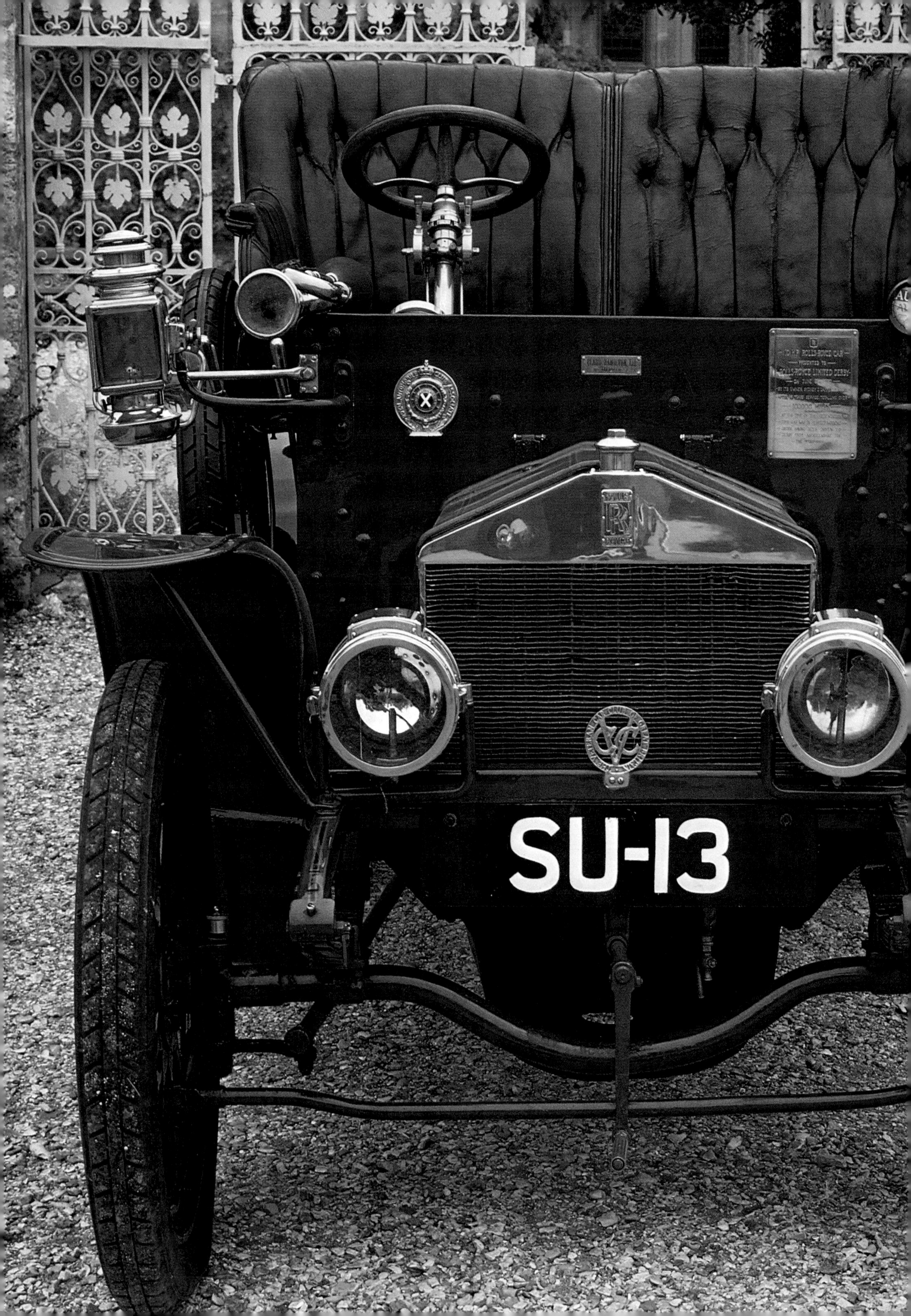
SU-13

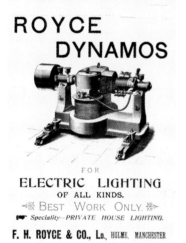

ROYCE
DYNAMOS

FOR
ELECTRIC LIGHTING
OF ALL KINDS.
❧ BEST WORK ONLY. ❧
☞ Speciality—PRIVATE HOUSE LIGHTING.

F. H. ROYCE & CO., Lᴅ., HULME, MANCHESTER

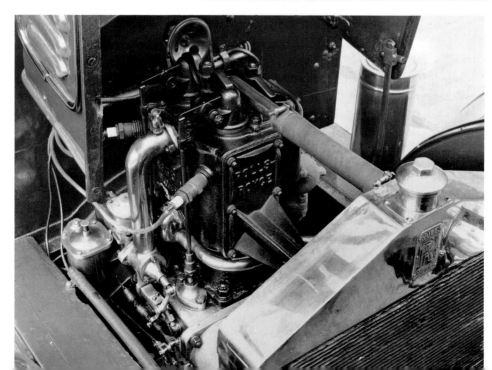

departed for South Africa with his wife (he and Claremont had married two sisters named Punt in 1893).

Royce returned refreshed and renewed but his doctor feared a relapse. He and Claremont thereupon talked him into buying a proper car (which the Quadricycle was not) that they hoped would get him out into fresh country air on weekends. They couldn't foresee that getting Royce involved with motorcars would soon set him to working harder than ever.

In the fall of 1902 Royce bought a used 10-hp, two-cylinder French Decauville. The Decauville wasn't too bad a car for its day. It was, in fact, better than most small two-cylinder machines of 1902. But like all such cars, it vibrated like Jell-O, made annoying noises, required much fiddling with ignition and carburetion levers, and was not too reliable.

Royce, the mechanical perfectionist, was sure that he could build a far better motorcar. Further, the crane and dynamo business wasn't quite what it had been. Shouldn't Royce Ltd. get into the burgeoning automobile business? Royce seems to have quickly convinced his associates that three experimental cars ought to be laid down, and early in 1903 he and a small group of draftsmen started making working drawings.

Henry Royce didn't merely hand the blueprints to a squad of machinists and say, "Here, build this car." Mostly he took off his coat and worked on the new cars himself with the help of two assistants.

Not surprisingly, Royce used much of the now-maligned Decauville as his model; he was never a great innovator. But he was a master craftsman with solid engineering instincts. He could make astonishing improvements on every mechanical and electrical device he examined.

The new Royce car was not revolutionary in overall design. What was revolutionary was the care in design of each individual component. Each part of the whole—the engine, the ignition system, the gearbox, and the rest—was better designed, better made, and more efficient than such elements ever had been. And they worked *quietly!* This was to be true of every Royce-designed car ever built. That was Henry Royce's real genius.

Those first Royces were simple little machines. Their two vertical cylinders (95-mm bore x 127-mm stroke) were rated at 10 hp. Pushrods operated the overhead inlet valves, which were set above the exhaust valves. And their exposed pushrods and rockers made nary a sound.

The engines' "breathing" was a great improvement over that in other early Edwardian machines, whose carburetors sent mixture to their cylinders through long and oddly convoluted piping and whose exhaust gases fought their way through ridiculously skinny tubes to inadequate mufflers. Royce's engine boasted sensibly straight manifolding and a huge muffler that did much for the engines' uncanny hush.

Royce was, of course, a master electrician. And the design of his ignition systems

Preceding pages: 1905 Rolls-Royce.
Opposite top: Charles Rolls driving the 1897
Léon Bollée tri-car. Middle left: 1890's
advertisement for Royce dynamos. Middle right: Chassis
of the first 1904 Royce car. Bottom: Two-cylinder
engine of the 1905 Rolls-Royce.

AS SILENT AS ITS SHADOW

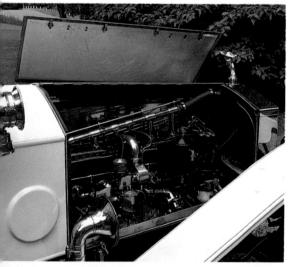

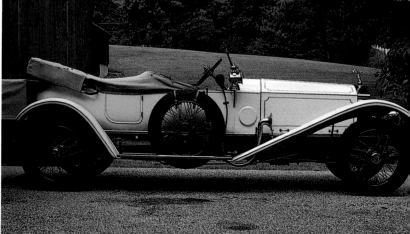

Connoisseurs love the sporting 1913
"London-Edinburgh"-type Rolls-Royce. The model was
based on a specially prepared machine that
did 78.26 mph and 24.32 miles per imperial gallon,
all in top gear, during the 1911 Royal Automobile
Club Test. Top left: Rolls ad of 1930's.

213

showed it. But it was in the superb finish and accuracy of the components, not in their originality, that the Royce touch showed. The experimental cars still used spark coils, as almost every other Edwardian car would do for years. And as in other machines power was transmitted through a leather-lined cone clutch. But Royce's clutches engaged smoothly and gently. Royce cars never started off with a neck-snapping leap.

Royce used an already obsolete kind of three-speed gear change, the progressive type, in which the gear lever moved along a quadrant. It was necessary to go through second gear if the driver wished to downshift from top gear into first gear. By 1903 most makers were already using the Mercedes type of selective gate change, with which any gear could be selected directly. Why did Royce use the older type? Evidently because that was what his Decauville had. As we might expect, however, the Royce gearbox made no unseemly grinding or howling sounds, merely a very light musical hum, thanks to supercareful fitting and gear-tooth design.

The first of the two-cylinder engines was tested on September 16, 1903. Ever the electrician and of an economical turn of mind, Royce ordered the engine coupled to one of his dynamos. Starting a newly designed engine is always a rather nervous proceeding. But after a couple of turns of the crank the engine came alive without drama. It ran for more than four hours at full bore while its gasoline consumption was recorded. Royce wanted to know how much the electricity it generated cost. It came out to not quite four cents per kilowatt hour. Royce wasn't entirely satisfied, and among other things changed the shape of the cams to give less lift.

Although everybody involved in building the new cars put in savagely long hours—starting time was 6:30 A.M., quitting time was as late as Royce insisted and often right through the night on Fridays—Royce himself worked even longer hours. It took six months after the first engine tests before the first Royce car took to the road. This slowness was due to Royce's fanatical insistence on perfection. Every part had to satisfy his incredibly high standards and components were tested, retested, and rebuilt.

If a workman was the least bit careless—if, for instance, he loosened a nut so that a cotter pin might be more easily fitted—Royce would blister him with a roar of street-learned profanity. Next time the poor fellow would file the nut so that the cotter-pin holes lined up when the nut was properly tightened.

On April 1, 1904, the first Royce car essayed a run on the streets of Manchester. A crude test body had been set on the chassis. Royce was at the wheel. A few pull-ups of the crank and the little engine gently started putt-putting away. As Royce slowly drove out the door all hell broke loose in the shop behind him. For he was noisily "hammered" out in the way young men who finished their apprenticeships in engineering shops were applauded—by everyone banging hammers on benches, floors, anvils, anything that would make a racket. Royce, slightly embarrassed but smiling confidently, then drove the 15 miles to his house at Knutsford, near Manchester. His associates apparently didn't share his confidence. The old Decauville was sent along behind the Royce.

But the first Royce car had no problems a little fiddling and fussing wouldn't put right. Within a week or so it went off to the coachbuilders for a proper body.

Royce now had a fine car that people would most certainly buy. But who would do the selling? A young man named Rolls, whom Royce had never heard of, would soon take care of that.

Charles Stewart Rolls was a young man of as different a background from Henry Royce as could possibly be. Born in 1877, he was the third son of the immensely rich Lord Llangattock and lived in a luxurious town house at Knightsbridge in London and at the family seat, "The Hendre," in Monmouth, near the Welsh border. The house sat on thousands of acres and had a front drive two miles long. One thousand head of deer ranged the park, while some four hundred servants took care of things. Eton and Cambridge were almost foreordained for young Rolls.

It is not too unusual for the sons of the very rich to be parsimonious. Rolls was remarkably so. The most he'd spend for lunch in a restaurant was tenpence, and he'd tip the waiter a penny. When involved with motorcars he dressed like a tramp.

While at Cambridge Rolls became fascinated with that new sport of the rich—motoring. He bought his first car, a 3½-hp Peugeot, in 1894. At first he ran it only when in France, for there were ridiculous restrictions against road vehicles in England, including a 4-mph speed limit. Soon, in an effort to get the archaic regulations changed, a group of rich men, including Rolls, intentionally broke the law. They succeeded, and on November 14, 1896, it became legal to drive a car in England at 12 mph. In that year, too, an exhibition of self-propelled vehicles (some of them could hardly be called cars) was held at the Imperial Institute in London. Helping to arrange this show was a superefficient young official of the Institute, Claude Goodman Johnson, who later did much to make the name of Rolls-Royce great.

Rolls meanwhile became a leading figure among the new breed of wild-eyed, wealthy automobilists. He raced, entered trials, involved himself in reliability runs, including the still-famous 1,000 Miles Trial of 1900, which Claude Johnson organized and in which Rolls performed brilliantly with his 12-hp Panhard et Levassor.

In 1903 Rolls and Johnson became partners in C. S. Rolls & Company, a car dealership purveying mostly Panhards and Minervas to Rolls's upper-crust friends. It wouldn't be long before Rolls would be selling them an even better make of car.

A man named Henry Edmunds, a director of Royce Ltd. and a motoring enthusi-

ast, decided that C. S. Rolls & Company were just the right people to sell Royce cars. But he had a bit of trouble. Royce wasn't anxious to travel to London to meet a toff like Rolls. Besides, he was busy putting together the third of his two-cylinder cars. Nor was Rolls crazy about going all the way to Manchester to have a man he'd never heard of show him another two-cylinder car that would most likely be too noisy and rough for his exalted clientele. But Edmunds was persuasive. Royce and Rolls met for lunch at the Grand Central Hotel in Manchester. Surprisingly, the gilded young man and the bluff engineer liked each other.

Rolls must have shown his disappointment when he first saw Royce's car, for it was a most unappealing-looking little device. Mechanically it was quite unoriginal in concept. And it still had an ugly round-topped shape to its radiator. (The classic Parthenon shape would come later.) Ah, but when Rolls drove it! He was entranced by its manner of going, its silent smoothness. Later he went around saying, "I have found the greatest motor engineer in the world!" So he had.

But Rolls still had reservations about two-cylinder cars, so it was agreed that Royce would also construct three-, four-, and six-cylinder machines. The virtues of six-cylinder machines were then being trumpeted by S. F. Edge, of Napier's, as *the* in thing, and Rolls wasn't about to be surpassed by the loud-mouthed Edge. Finally, after further meetings it was agreed that Royce Ltd. would make cars only for C. S. Rolls & Company. They would be known as Rolls-Royces.

By December, 1904, Royce was able to finish five Rolls-Royce cars to be exhibited at the prestigious Paris Salon. A two-cylinder, 10-hp chassis was gussied up for show and another two-cylinder machine was used as a demonstrator. A three-cylinder, 15-hp chassis, a complete four-cylinder, 20-hp car, and a six-cylinder engine were also shown.

By the early summer of 1905 Rolls & Company was able to sell all the cars that Royce could turn out in his small factory, which continued building electrical products. To publicize the cars Rolls entered two of the four-cylinder, 20-hp Rolls-Royces in the Tourist Trophy race. These were Light Twenties, specially tuned for the race. There were also Heavy Twenties, less suitable for competition and designed to carry ponderous formal coachwork.

The 208½-mile race was run on the Isle of Man on September 14, 1905, and the cars were allowed to have only 9¼ gallons of gasoline in their tanks. Sadly, Rolls had bad luck. Downshifting from overdrive fourth to third speed during the very first lap, "THERE WAS A CRACK, AND THE GEARS HAD PARTED," as *The Motor* magazine described it. The other Twenty, driven by Rolls demonstrator Percy Northey, did better. It finished second at 33.7 mph. An Arrol-Johnston came in first—at 33.9 mph.

A year later, Rolls won the TT.

In December, 1906, Rolls, while introducing the Rolls-Royce at the American Au-

Top: 1930 20/25-hp Rolls-Royce with "Foursome De Ville" body by Barker, the famous English coachbuilding firm that first built carriages in 1710. Bottom: Early Rolls-Royce Phantom I built in Springfield, Massachusetts. The "Piccadilly" roadster body is by Brewster. Note the typically American drum headlights and tubular bumper.

tomobile Club's New York show, raced a Light Twenty at the Empire City Track. He beat all comers in a 5-mile race. Later, upon his return to England, he quite tactlessly told some American reporters stationed in England of his low opinion of American cars. Infuriated, E. R. Thomas, the windy builder of the Thomas Flyer, immediately challenged Rolls to a race from New York to Chicago, insisting that it take place within thirty days. Another noisy gentleman, L. S. Perlman, the Welch agent from New York, echoed Thomas. It was obviously impractical for Royce to accept the thirty-day stipulation, but he invited them both to enter the TT. Neither did so.

By now there was no longer a C. S. Rolls & Company. A new company, Rolls-Royce Ltd., capitalized at £60,000, had been formed. But Royce Ltd., the electrical manufacturers, still remained.

In 1905 Royce made a mistake. He allowed himself to be talked into designing a most peculiar and gutless town carriage that would be as quiet and smooth as an electric. It would have its engine hidden under the floor so as not to irk the sensibilities of those who thought internal-combustion engines vulgar. And it would do no more than 20 mph in top gear. Hence its name: Legalimit. The invisible engine was a very flat V-8 with full-pressure lubrication to obviate smoke. Only one Legalimit was ever delivered (to Lord Northcliffe), and even this one was ordered with its engine out front under a very low, wide hood. Two more, with their engines under the floor, are known to have been built but scrapped. Rumors that others still exist have been around for years. If you find one your fortune will have been made.

The 30-hp, six-cylinder Rolls-Royce of 1905 was not nearly so bad a disaster as the Legalimit, but neither was it a triumph. The engine consisted of three two-cylinder units, each of which was adapted from the 10-hp, two-cylinder car (the four-cylinder Twenty used two sets of two-cylinder units). Thus the crankshaft was long and skinny and whippy. Con rods were long, too. Further, the problems of torsional vibration in six-cylinder engines were still insufficiently understood, even by Royce. Cars came back to the factory with broken crankshafts. Royce went back to the drawing board after only thirty-seven of the new sixes were built.

The 40/50-hp, six-cylinder Rolls-Royce (later known as the Silver Ghost) was about to be conceived. It would become "the Best Car in the World." Royce gave up the idea of using the same twin-cylinder blocks that had formed the engines of the four-cylinder Twenty and, in triplicate, the six-cylinder Thirty. He now used two three-cylinder blocks set back to back. The nickel-steel crankshaft was now unbreakably thick and massive, and the con rod and main bearings were now required to be nearly twice the diameter of those on the 30-hp six. Now, too, full-pressure lubrication was used. Unlike most cars of the period, the 40/50 did not lay down the usual smokescreen that occurred when drivers, fearful of starving their bearings, adjusted their oil drip-feeds to lubricate their engines too liberally.

The engine was an L-head and the head was not detachable. But Royce, perhaps showing off, did not enclose the valve gear. Royce knew that he did not need to cover it up to ensure silence. Superprecise fitting ensured that.

Ignition was by trembler coil and magneto with two spark plugs per cylinder. As was usual at the time, the coil ignition was used for starting, the magneto for running. Also, like other good-quality cars, if the engine had not stood for too long after having been run, it would "start on the switch" by merely turning on the coil ignition and moving the spark control on the steering wheel hub from "late" to "early" and back to "late." Unlike other makers, Royce never did mark his spark control "advance" and "retard."

Unlike most carburetors of 1907, the Royce-designed instrument, as beautifully and precisely made as a fine, polished brass microscope, gave the 40/50 amazing flexibility. It was one car whose driver did not have to fiddle continually with extra-air levers. There was, however, a hand control to enrich or weaken the mixture for starting or mountain climbing.

Although the 40/50's engine was silkily smooth, unbelievably quiet (for its day), and almost unbreakable, it delivered a laughable 48 hp at 1,250 rpm from its huge, 7,036-cc (114 x 114-mm) engine. Small valves, a narrow-throated carburetor, and overzealous muffling so restricted the engine's breathing that it was in effect always running at part throttle. Someone once cracked, "The 40/50 used thirty horsepower to quiet down the eighteen that moved it along."

The chassis was quite unremarkable except for the meticulous way in which it was built. The clutch was a leather cone, the gearbox had four speeds—the top one being an overdrive. And the frame was suspended on five leaf springs, one for each wheel and a fifth athwartships aft, a "platform" spring.

When I was last in London there stood in Rolls-Royce's Conduit Street showroom a most magnificent 40/50, the famous Silver Ghost that has now been driven upwards of half a million miles since it was built in 1907. This is the selfsame machine—the thirteenth 40/50 built—that publicity-wise Claude Johnson had fitted with touring coachwork painted silver. Its metal fittings were silver-plated. Johnson, who liked giving cars names as if they were ships, also ordered that a silver-plated plaque with the name "Silver Ghost" be fitted to the dashboard. The name stuck. Today we call all early 40/50's Silver Ghosts. It was with that first Silver Ghost that Johnson set out to make the name of Rolls-Royce great.

The Ghost was first entered in the Scottish Trials, then sent off to run for 15,000 miles nonstop (never on Sunday) day and night. It did stop once at the 629th mile, when a loose

gasoline tap shook itself shut. But its engine never stopped during its shuttling back and forth between Glasgow and London. When it at last stopped and was dismantled, nothing was worn enough to need replacement. But to make the car "showroom new" again, only £2 2s.7d. ($10.64) was spent on new parts.

In later years other Ghosts kept the name great. In 1911 S. F. Edge, who was, if anything, more publicity-minded than Claude Johnson, sent one of his Napiers on a run from London to Edinburgh in top gear only. Fuel consumption was measured and a high-speed run was made at Brooklands track. The Napier did 19.35 miles per (imperial) gallon, and 76.42 mph at Brooklands.

Johnson, not to be outdone, sent a Ghost on the same run. This machine—a special job with a tapered hood, a slightly higher compression (3.5 to 1 instead of 3.2 to 1), a wider-throated carburetor, and cantilever rear springs—did even better than the big Napier: 24.32 miles per (imperial) gallon and 78.26 mph. Later the "London-Edinburgh" model was offered to the public. If I could have my choice of Ghosts this is the one I'd love to own.

Soon afterward a "London-Edinburgh" with a light, streamlined, single-seat body did 101 mph for the quarter-mile at Brooklands. The Ghosts after 1909 had slightly bigger engines with half-inch-longer strokes: 7,428 cc instead of 7,036, and more power, too—60 bhp, still surprisingly low for their size. It was in 1909, too, that Claude Johnson convinced the other company directors that the 40/50 Ghost was the only model that ought to be made.

In July, 1910, Charles Rolls, who had first been a balloonist and then a flier, crashed his French-built Wright biplane and was killed. A year later, Royce had another collapse. This time cancer was diagnosed. He was successfully operated on but was an invalid for the rest of his life. Although he rarely came back to the factory, he continued to work with assistance in his villa at Le Canadel in the south of France in winter, and at his summer home in West Wittering, Sussex. He died in 1933.

It has been said, cruelly, that Royce's absence was good for the company. That his passion for perfection, his continual changes and improvements, slowed production and cost many thousands of pounds.

During those golden years before the Kaiser War, Rolls-Royce reached its apogee. The still-crowned heads of Europe, the nobility, the millionaires, just *had* to own Rolls-Royces. In those days the Rolls-Royce was indisputably "the Best Car in the World." After the war it still might be "best," but the gap between it and lesser cars would narrow and in some cases virtually disappear.

From 1914 to 1918 the big Rolls-Royce factory at Derby (to which the company had moved in 1907) was busy building airplane engines. But also built were those famous Rolls-Royce armored cars that served on every front from Russia to Palestine, from France to German West Africa. And those Ghost chassis, car-

Top: In 1911 a "London-Edinburgh"
Rolls-Royce fitted with a narrow single-seat body
covered a quarter-mile on Brooklands track at
101 mph. Bottom: Rolls-Royce armored cars
fought the Turk during World War I and the Nazis
in North Africa during the 1940's.

rying double the weight they were designed for (although on twin rear wheels), never faltered. No matter how rough the going, only bullets could stop them. And some of the same machines were brought out again to fight the Afrika Korps in the western desert in World War II.

After the Armistice the Ghost changed but little. Certainly, it now had electric lighting and starting, and aluminum pistons. The trembler coil was gone, too. The platform spring was long gone. And by 1923 it also had four-wheel brakes operated via a gearbox-energized servomechanism built under license from Hispano-Suiza.

The Silver Ghost had, of course, been much improved during its long life, but in 1925 it was still basically the car of 1906. Only the Model T Ford had lived as long. Other machines, notably the Hispano-Suiza H6 with its superb six-cylinder overhead-camshaft engine, had not only caught up with the Ghost but even surpassed it in some ways.

In 1925 the Silver Ghost was succeeded by the New Phantom. Later, when the New Phantom was itself superseded by the Phantom II, the New Phantom became known as the Phantom I. In essence, the New Phantom was a late Silver Ghost with a new engine. This now had overhead valves operated by pushrods, a detachable head and a smaller bore (108 mm), and a longer stroke (139.5 mm) than the Ghost's. Cubic capacity was 7,668 cc.

The Silver Ghost engine had peaked at only 2,250 rpm. At this engine speed the Phantom I was a third more powerful. At its peak engine speed of 2,750 rpm it was not only some 10 mph quicker than a Ghost but also accelerated much faster and climbed hills with more verve. Top speed was over 80 mph.

The Ghost's cone clutch was gone, too. No longer would it be necessary, when putting the car away, to keep the clutch pedal pushed down with a stick to prevent the leather surfaces from sticking. The Phantom now had a disc clutch.

I never owned a pukka English-built Phantom I. The two I owned were made in Springfield, Massachusetts. In 1920 Rolls-Royce of America, owned by American stockholders but mostly by Rolls-Royce Ltd. of England, set up shop in Springfield in a factory in which Indian motorcycles and, later, wire wheels had been manufactured. The American Rolls-Royce was *not* a British Rolls assembled in Springfield. Every one of its parts, except for the crankshaft, was American-made. At first it was almost identical to the Derby-built machine, but as time went on it differed more and more from its British sisters.

At first, naturally, the Springfield cars were Silver Ghosts. In fact the early ones even had right-hand steering. Left-hand drive wasn't fully standardized until 1924. This meant that the beautiful right-hand gear lever gave way to a central gear lever. The four-speed gearbox was no more. American Rollses had three-speed gearboxes. The coil-and-magneto ignition system was changed to twin coils. The starter and generator were built by Westinghouse instead of Rolls-Royce. American-built wire wheels replaced those previously made in England. And so on. Still, the Springfield machines were indubitably Rolls-Royces in feel and in look. And American coachwork, especially the Brewster bodies, was second to none.

Between 1921 and 1931, when production ended, 1,703 Silver Ghosts and 1,241 Phantom I's were built in Springfield. No Phanton II's were ever built there, despite the fact that the PII was already in production in England by 1929.

I got my first Phantom I in 1937 because its owner, a German-American mouth-organ manufacturer, liked Hitler and thought he ought to own a 540K Mercedes-Benz instead of a Rolls-Royce. Mercedes in New York refused to take the Rolls in trade, so I was able to buy it with a lovely primrose-and-black Brewster "Ascot" body for $275. Only 17,000 miles were on the clock. I owned that car for six years and thought it the greatest thing on wheels. It wasn't until much later, when I owned a couple of Phantom II's (in succession, not together), that I became critical, in retrospect, of my two PI's. (I acquired another one with a Brewster "Riviera" body in 1952.)

The Phantom I's were fairly fast—in the mid-80's—but were rather lumpish to drive. Their steering was heavy and their cantilever rear springing and torque-tube drive (inherited from the Ghost) didn't help their roadholding at high speed. Nor were their three-speed gear-boxes too pleasurable to handle. I must admit, however, that they were absolutely reliable and unbreakable. Nothing ever went wrong.

The Phantom I was produced for only a few years, from 1925 to 1929 (until 1931 in Springfield). In 1925 the Phantom I had been the answer to sophisticated new machines like the Hispano-Suiza. Now Rolls-Royce was being challenged by cars like the fast 6½-liter Bentley and the V-12 Daimler Double Six. What reasserted Rolls's leadership was the Phantom II, which first appeared at the London Motor Show in 1929. And in the view of this writer it was the greatest Rolls-Royce ever built. Like the PI (and the Silver Ghost) it had twin three-cylinder blocks, and also like the PI it had a cubic capacity of 7,668 cc. But Royce had redesigned the aluminum cylinder head. The intake and exhaust manifolds were now at opposite sides of the head for better breathing, especially at high speed.

The big change was in the chassis. It was now lower and more rigid. The cantilever rear springs gave way to semielliptics. The torque tube had been eliminated. The PII now had "Hotchkiss" drive. Wheelbase of the standard model was 150 inches. The short-chassis Continental model had a wheelbase that was six inches shorter.

Both of the PII's I had were Continentals. The first one was a Continental Touring Saloon with a four-passenger Park Ward body. It had had a hard life and I hadn't the wherewithal to set things right. I soon sold it.

I was luckier with my second one. I'd seen an advertisement in the Sunday New York *Times* for a PII Continental Rolls with a drophead body for a mere $1,000. The car was in Paris. On that particular Sunday the members of the Rolls-Royce Owners Club of America were far away in Montreal for a meet. I had no competition. Within weeks I drove the car home from the New York docks.

My car was a 1935 model (187 TA) with a four-passenger convertible body by Henry Binder of Paris. It was different from British-delivered Rolls-Royces in having its speedometer calibrated in kilometers and in the kind of auxiliary shock absorbers it had. In addition to their adjustable shock absorbers, sporting English Continentals had an extra set of friction shock absorbers to further stiffen their suspensions at high speed. These were activated hydraulically by André Telecontrols. My car had an extra set of Hartford-type friction shockers that were adjusted by means of a pair of tiny cranks under the steering wheel. The cranks tightened the shock absorbers via thin cables. All I ever had to do to that Rolls was replace the muffler (Rolls-Royce still had them in stock in 1959) and change the spark plugs.

The car was a delight on the road. It was quick: zero to 100 kph (62 mph) in nineteen seconds, top speed 160 kph (100 mph) on the speedometer. The steering was accurate, roadholding was excellent, though not exactly in the Alfa or Bugatti class. Although gear-shifting was almost redundant—British drivers habitually started in third speed—I used the lovely right-hand gear lever for the sheer sensual pleasure it gave me. It made not a sound as it moved silkily from notch to notch. On late PII's the synchromesh was faultless.

But my PII had its little faults. The one-shot lubrication system, which, at the touch of a plunger, was supposed to send oil down many yards of piping to ease various joints in the corpus of the Rolls, failed to send enough to the steering department. The kingpins turned less freely than they should have. The brake servo's discs, "designed to function without lubricant," somehow contrived to get themselves greasy. Rolls-Royce's London service depot would have taken care of the small defects in short order. But the New York agents couldn't be bothered. I still much regret that in a fit of pique I sold the machine.

The next in the Phantom line—the PIII—was built from 1936 until war ended the construction of such beautifully complex mechanisms forever. It was the first Phantom that was not built under the aegis of Sir Frederick Henry Royce.

The PIII had not only a V-12 engine, but also independent front suspension. For by the late thirties such a specification was *de rigueur* in luxury vehicles. The V-12 engine had a slightly smaller capacity than its forebears—7,338 cc—and pushrod-operated overhead valves with hydraulic tappets. Unlike those in Rolls-Royces of today, the PIII's engine and its electrical parts were made under Rolls-Royce's

Top: 1934 Rolls-Royce Phantom II Continental fitted with a Gurney Nutting Owen Sedanca coupe body. The short-chassis Continental model could exceed 90 mph. Bottom: This experimental Phantom I was one of several built in 1928 to test new features to be incorporated in the soon-to-come Phantom II.

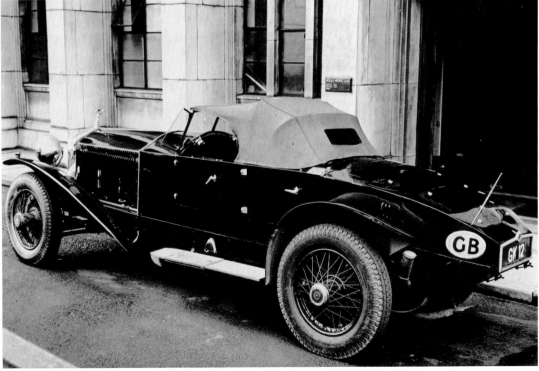

own roof. Only the carburetors were no longer of Rolls-Royce design. They were based on the American Stromberg.

Although no engine of its day ran more smoothly or was more lovingly finished, there were troubles in paradise. The hydraulic tappets stuck and tended to destroy the camshaft. And replacing a PIII's deeply buried camshaft could mean expensive surgery, even in the 1930's. The trouble was caused by dirt in the oilways. If the owner of a PIII followed the handbook's instruction about oil filters he had no difficulties. But few did. Further, if the kind of detergent oil we use today had been available there most likely wouldn't have been tappet trouble. In any event, R-R converted many cars to solid tappets. Others were botched by used-car pirates. After 1938 PIII's left the factory with solid tappets.

The PIII's independent front suspension was made under license from General Motors, but with Rolls-Royce workmanship and modifications. One modification caused a slight problem. The horizontally positioned coil springs were enclosed in oil-filled containers. After many miles the springs would sag a bit, touch the sides of the casing, and make un-Rolls-Royce-like graunchings.

The independent front suspension also caused the PIII to look rather clumsy and less pleasing than a Phantom II. This was because it now became possible to move the engine forward, over the suspension system. This had not been practical in earlier Phantoms, whose

long elegant hoods, set well back from the front wheels, gave them their uniquely patrician look. But moving the engine forward *did* give the passengers more room.

A PIII could really move! A big limousine-bodied 1939 model could exceed 100 mph and go from zero to 60 mph in seventeen seconds.

A Phantom III with its complexities can cost a fortune to maintain today. Merely changing its twenty-four spark plugs takes about five hours. At $20 per hour for labor—plus the cost of the plugs—it might come to . . . ?

After the Hitler War, Rolls-Royce built two further models that they called Phantoms, perhaps because the cars did not really fit in with the main line of Rolls-Royce produc-tion. The first of these machines, the Phantom IV, was built in 1950 exclusively for royalty and heads of state. Only sixteen were built. Besides going to the inmates of Buckingham Palace, they went to such worthies as Generalissimo Francisco Franco, the Emir of Kuwait, and various other Arab potentates. The Phantom IV was the only straight-eight Rolls ever built. Its engine was a big F-head (inlet over exhaust), 5,675-cc cast-iron affair from the B series Rolls had originally built for military use during World War II. A four-cylinder version of this engine had gone into the Jeep-like Austin Champ. The six-cylinder version powered the Mark VI Bentley and Rolls-Royce's 1947–1959 Silver Wraith. The straight eight had been used in army vehicles.

Left: 1927 American-built Phantom I
Rolls-Royce with "Ascot" phaeton body by Brewster.
The author often drove this 5,000-pound machine
at over 80 mph. The car was bought in 1937
for $275, sold in 1942 for $400. It's worth rather more
today. Right: 1934 Phantom II Rolls-Royce.

The Phantom V (and its updated 1972 version, the Phantom VI), first built in 1959, was also a vast equipage designed for formal use. This one, powered by a 6,230-cc V-8 engine, had a Rolls-Royce version of the General Motors Hydramatic transmission. A friend once had me transported to an airport in one of these royal barges. It was notably quick and luxuriously comfortable. But I felt oddly lonesome in a rear compartment as spacious as a small ballroom.

Present-day Rolls-Royces and Bentleys are not descended from the 40/50-hp Silver Ghost and the 40/50-hp Phantoms I and II. They have a rather smaller ancestor, the 20-hp "Baby Rolls" of 1923. Royce, it is said, designed the smaller Rolls because he feared that the post-World War I slump would require a less expensive machine, a car designed for the owner-driver. It turned out to be not so cheap: £1,590 ($7,950) with an open touring body. Such a price was perhaps not unexpected, since it was built to Royce's fanatically high standards.

The "Baby" had a six-cylinder, pushrod-operated, overhead-valve engine of 3,150 cc, which developed some 50 bhp. It was the first Rolls engine to have a detachable head. Its bigger sister, the Silver Ghost, which was still in production, had torque-tube drive and rear cantilever springs, but the Twenty had Hotchkiss drive and semielliptics aft. It was the new car's gearbox that infuriated British purists. It had only three speeds, and those were selected by a central gear lever springing from a ball on the floorboards, a downright revolting American practice. The Twenty wasn't any powerhouse. Sixty mph was about as fast as it could be made to go. But it could proceed at a walking pace if its driver were too lazy to shift down. It was a lovely car for pottering along on twisting English lanes.

In 1925 Henry Royce gave in to the carpers. The Twenty now had a four-speed gearbox with its control lever on the right, "where it belonged." Over the years the Twenty grew up and got more muscle. It became the 20/25 in 1929, the 25/30 in 1936, the Wraith in 1939.

In 1931 Rolls-Royce bought the assets of Bentley Motors Ltd., outmaneuvering their ancient competitors, Napier, who were about to take over the builders of those champions of Le Mans. The first Rolls-built Bentley, "the silent sports car" that appeared in 1933, had a 3½-liter engine derived from that in the 20/25. But it was somewhat more sporting. Instead of the Rolls's single carburetor it had twin S.U.'s and a newly designed higher-compression head. It produced about 105 hp. The engines of the later 4¼-liter models of 1936 developed circa 125 hp. But the new Bentley had a chassis quite unlike that of the 20/25. It was based on an experimental frame intended for a new small 2¾-liter Rolls-Royce that had never been produced.

If not in the tradition of the hairy-chested thunderers beloved by the Bentley Boys, the new Bentleys were indeed lovely sporting machines with a top speed of 95 mph and zero-to-60 times of about sixteen seconds. I could, however, always run away from a 4¼ Bentley in my Invicta.

Rolls-Bentleys hadn't been built for racing. Yet E. R. Hall modified several of them and entered them privately in three Tourist Trophy races. He made the fastest time in every race but never placed better than second because of handicapping. In 1935, in a 3½-liter, he averaged 80.36 mph for 478 miles, beating Lord Howe in a 3.3-liter Bugatti.

In 1939, land-speed record driver George Eyston covered 114.7 miles in one hour on Brooklands track. He accomplished this with a Mark V Bentley. This model, with independent front suspension, never got into full production. Only some twenty were built before World War II began. A prototype Corniche model, based on the Mark V, with a body built by Van Vooren that had been put through an endurance test in France, was wrecked at Dieppe by German bombs as it was about to be shipped to England.

About twenty years ago I owned a 4¼ (B175 LE) with a fairly heavy Thrupp and Maberly drophead body. It just wasn't nervous enough to really be called a sports car and had a tendency to wag its tail when cornering. But it was most pleasant as a fast tourer. If it hadn't continually broken its valve springs I might still be its happy owner. And I imagine it's now worth several times the $2,500 I sold it for.

After World War II it was obviously economically impossible for Rolls-Royce to build the kinds of cars they'd been building in the 1930's. A PIII that might have cost $25,000 with a bespoke body in 1939 would have to sell for well over $100,000 today—if you could find the craftsmen to build such bodywork. So the standard bodies for postwar Rolls-Royces were mostly pressed steel, although those for some postwar Wraiths and Bentleys—the Bentley Continental, for example—were still made to order.

Rolls-Royce no longer makes almost every single part of the cars it sells. Carburetors, radiators, ignition parts, generators, and starters were once made in its own factory. Today all such components are bought outside. In fact, even engine castings are "bought out." But Rolls-Royce is still unique in the way it makes and tests its cars. No other car factory in the world is so fussy. During a visit to the factory at Crewe a few years ago I asked the factory manager how many cars had been turned out that day. "We finished five," he said, "but the bloody testers brought every one back."

Every engine is brutally tested, first on a test stand. Using cooking gas for fuel, it is run for thirty minutes at idling speed, then another thirty minutes at moderate speed, and finally for four hours at revolutions equal to those it would attain in a car at fast cruising speed. Further, an engine is taken at random from each group that is finished and is run on gasoline for twenty-four hours at varying speeds, including its top-rated revolutions. It is then taken to bits right down to its smallest bolts and nuts, and

2

3

each part is carefully examined and measured. If any part shows the least sign of wear, or fatigue from stress or heat, the rest of the engines in the group are held back and minutely examined. At times one unlucky engine is chosen at random and is run long enough and fast enough to destroy itself. Then the boffins from the experimental department have a fine time figuring out what broke first and why.

Chassis frames are similarly torn to pieces and tested. Steering components, gears, and transmissions are run in to a condition of glassy smoothness before being installed in cars. Steering gears are tortured by smashing the front wheels against concrete blocks for thirty hours. If they do not then meet standard measurements of toe-in, caster, and camber they are rejected.

At Crewe I watched sharp-eyed gentlemen examining some newly delivered bodies. The bodies looked perfect to me. But the inspectors found near-invisible little dings and imperfections, around which they drew chalk rings.

Rolls-Royce interior coachwork is, expectedly, impeccable. But it was not the Circassion walnut-veneered instrument panels, the fancy carpeting, or the perfect seating that impressed me. What really amazed me was the lady who was sewing tiny leather caps to finish off the ends of the leather piping around the seats.

Since World War II the Silver Wraith, the Silver Dawn, and the Silver Cloud I, all with six-cylinder engines, the V-8-engined Silver Clouds II and III, and the Silver Shadows (which first appeared in 1967) have kept up the Rolls-Royce tradition of continual modification and improvement.

Today's 6,750-cc, V-8-engined Silver Shadow II and its super-deluxe versions, the Corniche and the Pininfarina-styled Camargue, obviously have every modern amenity (even sensors to measure outside air temperature in order to warn the driver of ice on the road). As in other luxury cars, the driver and passengers are ensconced in a cocoon of comfort. The temperature inside the car is always perfect, whether traversing central Alaska or central Africa. The passengers' posteriors have no knowledge of the bumpy realities of the highway. Nor do the hands of the man holding the steering wheel know much about the traumas and attitudes of the front wheels. I am afraid that the modern Rolls-Royce is almost as characterless as any Cadillac, although it is surely far more durable.

From the point of view of the present-day Rolls-Royce buyer (and there are more of them than ever before), the Rolls-Royce is better than ever. But what would Henry Royce think about a gearbox sump stamped out of tin plate? Still, Rolls-Royce does have links with its past. A school of instruction on the maintenance of Rolls-Royce cars still exists at Hythe Road in London. Although mostly for chauffeurs, private owners are also admitted.

And that "Grecian" radiator shell is still soldered together by hand.

Preceding pages: 1. 1952 Bentley with body by Freestone and Webb. 2. 1938 4¼-liter Bentley with Thrupp and Maberly body. 3. 1956 Hooper-bodied Bentley. 4. Bentley Continental by Mulliner. Opposite: Rolls-Royce Corniche convertible and Silver Shadow II. Following pages: 1978 Rolls-Royce Camargue.

Index

Italic numbers refer to illustrations

237

Picture Credits

RS—Ralph Stein
HAC—Harrah's Automobile Collection, Reno, Nevada
(Names in parentheses refer to car owners.)
Cover—RS (Miles Coverdale).
Alfa Romeo 12-13: RS (National Motor Museum, England). 16: (top) Alfa Romeo Archives; (btm) RS. 18: *The Autocar*. 20: (both) Alfa Romeo Archives. 22: RS. 24: RS. 26: (top) Alfa Romeo Archives; (btm) RS. 28: (top) RS; (mid & btm) Detroit Public Library. 32-33: (both) RS (Luigi Chinetti). 34: (all) Alfa Romeo Archives. 36: Alfa Romeo Archives. 37: (top) RS (Bob Grossman); (btm) Alfa Romeo Archives. 40-41: RS (Albert Squillace).
Duesenberg 44-45: RS (HAC). 48-49: (all) RS (HAC). 50-51: (all) Detroit Public Library. 52: (all) RS (HAC). 55: (top) HAC; (btm) Detroit Public Library. 57: (both) RS (Dieter Holterbosch).
Bugatti 60-61: RS (Miles Coverdale). 64-65: RS (Miles Coverdale). 66-67: H. G. Conway. 69: (both) RS (HAC). 70-71: (both) Author's collection. 72-73: (top left, btm left, top rt) RS (HAC); (btm rt) HAC. 76: (top) RS (HAC); (btm) RS (Miles Coverdale). 80: RS (Miles Coverdale). 82: RS. 85: (both) RS (HAC). 87: Author's collection. 88-89: RS (HAC).
Mercedes-Benz 92-93: RS (Dieter Holterbosch). 96: (all) Mercedes-Benz Archives. 98: (top left & rt, mid) Mercedes-Benz Archives; (btm) Author's collection. 100: (both) RS (HAC). 104: Author's collection. 105: (top left) Author's collection; (top rt & mid) RS (HAC); (btm) RS (Dieter Holterbosch). 106: (all) Mercedes-Benz Archives. 108-109: RS (Chris Noyes). 112-113: (both) Mercedes-Benz Archives.
Ferrari 116-117: RS (HAC). 120: (top) RS; (btm) RS (Bob Zambelli). 121: (both) RS (Luigi Chinetti). 122: (both) *Road and Track*. 124: (top & mid) RS (Luigi Chinetti); (btm) RS (Chinetti International Motors). 126: (top) *Road and Track*; (btm) Detroit Public Library. 127: Detroit Public Library. 128-129: (all) RS (Chinetti International Motors).
Bentley 132-133: RS (Maurice Schwartz). 136: RS (William Johnson). 138-139: (both) Author's collection. 140: (top) Author's collection; (btm) RS (Maurice Schwartz). 141: RS (National Motor Museum, England). 144: Author's collection. 145: RS (National Motor Museum, England). 146: (top) RS; (btm) Bentley Drivers' Club. 147: Bentley Drivers' Club. 148: RS (Dieter Holterbosch). 153: RS (National Motor Museum, England).
Hispano-Suiza 156-157: RS (Dieter Holterbosch). 160: (top left) *Autosport*; (top rt) Alex Ulmann; (btm left & rt) RS. 164: RS (John Sebert). 165: (top rt) RS (National Motor Museum, England); (btm) RS (John Sebert). 166-167: (top) Detroit Public Library; (btm) Author's collection. 169: (top) RS (Joseph Weider); (btm) HAC.
Maserati 172-173: RS (Jerry Mason). 176: (top, mid left, btm) Maserati Archives; (mid rt) Author's collection. 178: (both) Maserati Archives. 180: (top) RS; (btm) RS (Bob Grossman). 183: (top) Maserati Archives; (btm) Maserati Automobiles, Inc. 184-185: (top) Maserati Automobiles, Inc.; (btm) RS (Jerry Mason).
Isotta Fraschini 188-189: RS (HAC). 192: RS (HAC). 195: (top & mid) Detroit Public Library; (btm left & rt) RS. 196: (both) Author's collection. 200-201: (both) RS (HAC).
Rolls-Royce 204-205: RS (Presley Blake). 208-209: (all) RS (National Motor Museum, England). 210: (top & mid left) Author's collection; (mid rt & btm) Rolls-Royce Ltd. 212-213: (top left) Author's collection; (all others) RS (Curtis Blake). 216: (top) RS (Theodore Mintz); (btm) RS. 220: (both) Rolls-Royce Ltd. 225: (both) Rolls-Royce Ltd. 226: RS. 227: RS (David Mathewson). 230-231: (mid left) RS; (all others) Rolls-Royce Ltd. 232: (both) Rolls-Royce Ltd. 234-235: Rolls-Royce Ltd.